# THE VIRGIN INTERNET
## RESEARCH GUIDE

# THE VIRGIN INTERNET
# RESEARCH GUIDE

## VERSION 1.0

Simon Crerar

*Virgin*

First published in Great Britain in 2000 by
Virgin Publishing Ltd
Thames Wharf Studios
Rainville Road
London
W6 9HA

Version 1.0 – September 2000

A catalogue record for this book is available from the British Library.

ISBN 0 7535 0498 7

Designed and typeset by John and Orna Designs, London
Printed and bound by Omnia Books Ltd, Glasgow

# //STILL HAVEN'T FOUND WHAT YOU'RE LOOKING FOR?

The Internet is the world's largest library-cum-museum, containing millions of books, artefacts, images, documents and maps. But for many of its users, there is one small problem: everything is scattered about on the floor, with hordes of bewildered people frantically shifting through the mess, occasionally crying out, 'Wow! Look what I've found.'

While the net is now the serious researcher's first port-of-call for every type of information – and nowhere else lets you access such a tremendous range of material – if you've tried looking for something, you've probably realised that finding it is not as easy as you think. But providing you follow some simple principles, Internet research really can deliver what you're looking for. Whether you're doing academic research, searching for the latest long-range weather forecast or wanting to consult government databases, this book shows how easy it is to make the Internet your primary search tool.

Information accessed via the Internet has a vital advantage over books, magazines and newspapers: because it exists in digital form, it can be regularly updated, so you should never again feel you are consulting out-of-date material. Not only can you get news reports as they happen – from sources previously off limits to everyone save news journalists – you can use fast, sophisticated databases to find published information that would take you weeks to track down any other way.

The Internet is unconstrained by the concept of space. Your ability to be informed is only curtailed by your needs, rather than by the end of a TV programme or last page of a book or newspaper. The net doesn't make you wait for the next instalment or magazine publication date: it's always there, and always on. Because everyone can make a contribution, it contains as many points of view as there are opinions on Earth, and its very size makes it likely that you will find more detail or a more concise, understandable explanation if the first one leaves you baffled.

This new medium has thrown out long-accepted conventions about how we get our information. What once had to be paid for is now often free. Providers are falling over themselves to put every fact you will ever need at your fingertips. Entire books and whole encyclopedias, vast photo, video and audio libraries, all kinds of magazines, and even legal records and in-depth company information are all available, and you'll be amazed how easy it is to access them.

Students swotting for exams will find reference works they can trust from leading authorities. Small investors who want to check up on companies before committing precious cash will find all the background details they need to make informed, balanced decisions. And if you want to research something esoteric or obscure, chances are you'll be able to track down an enthusiast somewhere in the world who knows more than you do. The medium's origins as an academic information exchange have left a remarkable legacy; communities have formed for every research, study and hobby group imaginable.

Professional researchers are experts on different information systems and the ways they can be manipulated to get them what they want. They will not be deterred if their first attempt fails, because they have a range of alternative strategies to get what they want. But the rest of us can feel that we are wandering aimlessly through a maze of data. This book will show you the expert skills necessary to find exactly what you want, every time.

Above all, we've done as much of the research as possible ourselves. You'll find a comprehensive list of websites which cover all manner of commonly researched subjects.

- The school-boy looking for help with that all-important project,

- His big sister working out where to go on her gap year,

- Mum trying to find a recipe for that wok she got at Christmas,

- Dad attempting to get a grip on Asian technology markets,

- Granny worrying about sorting out a new motor insurance policy, and

- Grandpa trying to locate old buddies

– this book will help them all to find what they want.

Searching for information is more an art than a science, with the same query producing wildly different results depending on what search engine you choose. Many Internet users are tired of keying in a request to a search engine and getting back hundreds of suggestions, all completely unrelated to what you were really looking for. The aim of this book is to put a stop to that. Keep it by your PC – and cut out hours of frustration.

For his weekly *Webwatch* column in the London *Sunday Times*, Simon Crerar's mission is to explore the furthest-flung corners of the net in search of all manner of gems. In the process he has discovered everything there is to know about Internet research.

The Internet is a fluid, ever-changing medium. While this guide tries to recommend the kind of dependable sites that will still be going a decade from now, if a page appears a little different from how it is described or has inexplicably disappeared, please accept our apologies – and let us know by emailing us at **response@virgin-pub.co.uk**.

# //CONTENTS

## 1//THE INFORMATION REVOLUTION 1

A bit of background, and some Internet research basics.

## 2//SEARCH SECRETS 13

In-depth analysis of those all-important search engines.

## 3//HELPING HANDS 39

Where to find real live people to help with your enquiry.

## 4//GENERAL DIRECTORY 60

Start your research here, with links to the best places to look for information – divided by category.

# 1//THE INFORMATION REVOLUTION

The Internet has justly been called the most revolutionary information tool since Johann Gutenberg's printing press in the 15th century. Before the press, scribes had to copy out entire books by hand – a lengthy, laborious, expensive and mistake-prone process. Publishing was controlled by the governments and monasteries that employed the scribes. Gutenberg's press, on the other hand, had moveable letters that could be quickly and cheaply rearranged to print many error-free copies of any book. While few people knew how to read, the printing press nevertheless enabled ideas and knowledge to spread across Europe as never before. By making Scripture and commentaries more widely available, it helped to spark off the Reformation – a revolutionary popular challenge to the established church. Later, it made possible the period of scientific and intellectual change called the Enlightenment, and eventually our own age of mass literacy and education.

It's not clear whether the Internet will have similar far-reaching historical significance, but there is already some evidence that by making all kinds of information and opinion available to anyone with access to a PC, consumer choice and 'people power' are increasing. We are living through a sea change in information storage from the printed word to electronic records that are accessible everywhere, to anyone.

One thing's for sure: the Internet is the first new mass medium since television. And the technology is still in its infancy. There are boundless possibilities, many of which are undeveloped or even unimagined as yet. Meanwhile the web is doing its best to assimilate other media within it. You'll find that newspapers and many magazines are reproducing their entire content on the net, radio stations around the world are putting their broadcasts online in real time, news reports are webcast and musicians and filmmakers are using the net as their primary distribution method. To understand more about the Internet, and find out about its advantages and its limitations, it's worth a quick look at its background and evolution.

## A brief history

The Internet began as a computer network, set up in the USA during the 'Cold War' years of nuclear standoff between the USA and Soviet Russia. It was designed to let scientists and defence departments easily exchange information and keep in contact, and was set up to survive nuclear war in two important ways. First, it had no single, central computer that an enemy could take out in a missile strike. Secondly, information travelling across the network could take any route to its destination, so that if enemy action eliminated one set of cables or satellites, the data would simply seek another way through.

The Internet began in 1969, when the US Defense Advanced Research Projects Agency (DARPA) set up a project called Resource Sharing. At this early stage the Internet consisted of a series of linked mainframes passing basic messages and files using a method called packet switching. Data was spilt up into small parcels, each of which carried the name and address of its intended recipient. If one part of the network failed, the packet would simply take an alternative route until it reached its destination. Packets were then reassembled in the right order when they reached the receiving computer.

In 1973, DARPA began investigating different ways to join up the separate computer networks run by different military establishments. The aim was to develop protocols and procedures that all the computers would understand so that they could talk to each other. DARPA scientists Vint Cerf and Bob Khan developed the languages and conventions – called Transmission Control Protocol (TCP) and Internet Protocol (IP) – that are still used by every computer to access the Internet. And the Internet remains, in essence, the same now: a network of networks that can deliver packets of digital data (such as emails, pictures, software or web pages) anywhere in the world in less than a second.

When Britain's Queen Elizabeth sent the first royal email message in 1976, the Internet was still primarily a military network. But because many military contractors had academic backgrounds, they began to campaign for access for their research peers who remained offline. In 1984, after years of lobbying, the US National Science Foundation (NSF) network was created – as an academic version of the military network. From the beginning those connected began working to connect others.

By 1988 the NSF had a national system that enabled most university computers to communicate with each other. The net was still dominated by academics and scientists connected to university mainframes rather than personal computers. Twenty countries were connected to the NSF backbone, and those in the know anticipated that explosive growth was imminent. Companies began to offer commercial information online and services such as CompuServe enabled members of the public to hook their PCs up to the Internet via ordinary telephones.

In those days there were several methods of sharing or sending information over the Internet. People could email documents to each other or post them to bulletin boards where they could be seen by anyone. They could subscribe to a 'newsgroup' for a particular subject using a system called Usenet, whereby emailed postings would be passed around localised stores until the information was shared by them all. Or they could search directories of files held in centralised archives and download them using File Transfer Protocol (FTP). Each system had its own rules and its own software.

**Chapter 1//3**

## Enter the Web

Meanwhile British physicist Tim Berners-Lee, working at the European nuclear research centre (CERN) in Switzerland, invented a new communications system designed to help scientists to share particle physics research. Berners-Lee's big idea was that computer files held in different universities and research centres could be cross-referenced to each other by 'hypertext links' (or hyperlinks). A footnote in an essay, for example, would not just tell you the name and author of a learned article: it would contain a hyperlink that could be used to fetch the whole article from the computer that stored it.

Berners-Lee announced his system, which he called 'World Wide Web', in 1989. Three new pieces of software made up his proposal. Briefly, these were the easy-to-use HyperText Markup Language (HTML) used to write web documents, HyperText Transfer Protocol (HTTP) which transmits the pages between computers, and a 'web browser' program to receive, interpret and display the data transmitted. These systems were designed to work on any kind of computer, which has been a huge factor in the web's success. Today's web is very different from Berners-Lee's original, but it remains true to his vision in at least one respect: it's an enormous amount of information content connected by an enormous number of hypertext links.

Initially all HTML code documents were stored on one computer at CERN. The physicists called this computer a web server because it served-up groups of linked documents. By the end of 1992 there were more than 50 servers, mainly located at universities and research centres. Today there are an estimated three million servers around the world.

Because of these origins, and because anyone can contribute their own information (or disinformation), there is no single centralised database like you would find in a library, and no single catalogue of its contents. The Internet's great strength, its tremendous range of material, is also its biggest weakness – the medium is defiantly unstructured. No two sites arrange their information in the same way, which can make it a frustrating business finding what you want. Instead there are organised tools called search engines to help you. You'll find a lot more about these in Chapter 2.

**Internet research basics**

Before you set out to search the Internet, here's some essential advice on how to approach online research, whether to trust what you find and how to keep track of the sites you will be discovering.

**Don't be intimidated** by its size or the technology. People refer to Internet searching as looking for a needle in a haystack. Although there are more than a billion pages out there, and they're doubling every twelve months, finding what you want is easy if you master the basics of how to use your browser and the search engines. The nuts and bolts of the Internet are hidden behind the straight-forward interface of your browser. So don't get bogged down trying to understand how the information is transmitted around the world.

**Use your bookmarks.** Website addresses (or URLs) can be hard to remember, especially beyond a site's homepage, and mistyping a URL can often take you somewhere totally unexpected. Thankfully the major browsers offer similar services to keep track of the most useful sites. Internet Explorer (IE) has 'favorites' and Netscape Navigator 'bookmarks'. Whenever you find a site that you think is useful save it in your favorites. In IE, go to the Favorites menu and click Add to Favorites. In Navigator, go to the Bookmark menu and click Add Bookmark or File Bookmark. Add Bookmark puts the new bookmark at the bottom of the main Bookmarks list; File Bookmark lets you put the new bookmark into a separate subfolder. The Internet is huge, and it can be very difficult to find your way back to what you stumbled on before, so if you find something good, save it.

**Follow the links.** Any text on a page that is underlined is called a link (or hyperlink). If you move your cursor over it you'll see the cursor change to a small pointing hand. A mouse click will activate the link and take you the page, which could be part of the same website or somewhere else altogether. These links will often reveal specialist material you would never have found using a search engine or other method.

**Open pages in new windows.** This is especially useful if you are checking sites returned by a search engine, or if you think you will want to come back to the page you've just come from. So that you can consult more than one page at the same time, open new pages in separate windows. In both IE and Navigator, you right-click on the link (or hold down the mouse button if you are using a Mac) and then choose Open in New Window from the drop-down menu. However, the more windows you open, the slower your PC will be – and the more likely it is to freeze or crash. We don't recommend having more than five windows open at a time.

**Be specific.** Narrow down your search rather than wasting time with a broad subject wide enquiry. If you printed out the entire billion or so web pages now available on normal office paper, it would make a pile 70 miles high. With so much to choose from, be as specific as possible and you'll find what you want far quicker. For example, if you are looking for opening times at the Royal Botanical Gardens in Kew, London, you are more likely to find your answer if you search for 'Kew Gardens' than for 'opening times'.

**Is online research the right approach?** Believe it or not, it's often easier to find out the old-fashioned way. If you're looking for the telephone number of the local swimming pool, it's probably going to be quicker looking in the phone book than booting up your computer, logging on to the Internet and searching an online phone directory.

**Be sceptical.** There are no middlemen checking whether information on the web is even-handed or accurate. You could be tapping into the experience of an acknowledged expert in the field you are examining, or the site you are referring to could have been made as part of a senior school project. Or it could be a misleading spoof. It can be hard to judge a site's credentials, but you'll often find a page called About Us which explains who is behind the site. If there isn't a page like this, then it's up to you to decide whether the site should be trusted. As a general rule of thumb, you are safer with a source you already know and trust. Stock market data from the Motley Fool (**www.fool.com**) or the *Financial Times* (**www.ft. com**) is more reliable than information from a personal home page called Bob's Share Tips.

**Check the date.** It's easy to put information up online, but far harder to keep it maintained and updated. Some web pages seem to have been unchanged for years, and if you are looking for relevant and usable information this isn't going to help. When you arrive at the site, take a minute to find out whether the information has recently been updated – many pages have a 'this page was last updated on' message at the bottom of their homepage. A remarkable number of websites are still online despite being effectively defunct. Take a look at **www.ghostsites.com**, which shows you what to look out for.

**You might have to register or pay.** Not everything out there is free. Many sites (including most newspapers) make you register before letting you use them; you are then given an access password that you must key in each time you visit. Other sites are subscription only or charge you each time you use the service or take an item. If the quality of information merits payment, you may have to get your credit card out.

**If at first you don't succeed ...** try, try and try again. No single search engine or directory covers anything like the whole Internet. If you are looking for something specific, you're probably going to try some different approaches. By varying your search terms and using different methods, you stand a better chance of making a research breakthrough. There's a lot more about this in chapters 2 and 3.

**Use this book.** We've done a lot of the work for you. Whatever you're looking for, see if the subject area is covered in the later chapters of this book. If it is, then you are initially better off using one of these tailored sites than making an enquiry through a general-purpose search engine.

### The rest of this book

As you'd expect, research on the Internet usually starts with those all-important search engines. Chapter 2 shows you how to use search engines and directories to find exactly what you are looking for.

In the real world we also gather much of our information by talking to other people and asking questions. The Internet is no different – although the communication structure obviously is. Chapter 3 explains how to tap into the vast amount of dialogue taking place all the time online. Find out how to gossip and ask questions online, and how to use email to help your research.

You'll find the main directory of sites in Chapter 4. Divided into more than 50 topics, this comprehensive research guide covers everything from antiques to weather, and includes the Internet's best sites for finding the information you need in each category.

Chapters 5 and 6 cover educational and business research, two vast areas where the quantity and quality of material deserves separate coverage. More and more people are using the Internet to track down relatives and ancestors: Chapter 7 is your definitive introduction to genealogical research. You'll find technical terms explained at the back of the book. If at any stage you can't find what you are looking for, try the Index.

This Guide assumes that you have a computer which connects to the Internet and that you know how to use one of the major browsers to find a website. You should by now understand the basics of browsing and linking between sites, and will probably be familiar with the names of a couple of search engines – even if you can never get them to find anything you want.

If you're unclear about any of these points we recommend the companion volume to this book, **The Virgin Guide to the Internet**, which clearly explains how to go about getting a connection and familiarise yourself with the basic programs.

## //ADDRESS BOOK

### Starting points

*To get the ball rolling, try these general research guides. They are often the best places to start your research, especially if you've got a broad enquiry and want to learn more about a particular area. They provide excellent direction and support for all levels of experience.*

**4anything.com**                                    **www.4anything.com**
Vast network of more than 1,000 sites does a good job pointing you to the best of what is out there, easily and without fuss. Professional, full-time editors search through thousands of sites related to the topic you are interested in, so you don't have to. They then hand-pick seventy or eighty of the best links and post them on the site. You can guess a 4anything.com address (like **www.4cooking.com or www.4writing.com**) or search from this homepage.

**AskScott**                                          **www.askscott.com**
Scott Nicholson is a Texan librarian, and at the site you give his virtual alter ego basic information about what you're looking for. Just as a skilled librarian helps you find the right reference book, Ask Scott helps you find the most appropriate Internet sites for your search. The appeal of this site is its personal approach – it's

very obviously an individual effort, and this makes you feel like you are really getting what you want.

### The Argus Clearinghouse                    www.clearinghouse.net

Styling itself (not entirely accurately) as the Internet's main research library, this site provides a central access point for other websites that describe and evaluate information on the Internet. Only sites that pass a rigorous selection process are included, and they're all rated according to the quality of the material and the way it is organised. Each featured site is rated out of five, but the accompanying reviews can be less than informative.

### Internet Public Library                    www.ipl.org

The librarians strike back. The vast IPL is committed to providing free services to the Internet community. The site is brilliantly organised and logically arranged, managing to bring a semblance of order out of the net's chaos by selecting, evaluating and clearly describing the best of the web. Click on the Reference Center for a series of categories that take you to more and more specific information.

### LibrarySpot                    www.libraryspot.com

This virtual library resource centre – regularly selected by *Forbes* magazine as its best reference site – makes a good job of breaking through the information overload of the web, bringing researchers links to more than 5,000 online libraries and reference sites. Almost everything is immediately accessible from the intuitive, option-packed home page, including literary criticism, periodicals and online texts, government information, maps and encyclopedias.

### Refdesk                    www.refdesk.com

Back when the web was born, all sites were like this one – uncluttered by advertising, and lovingly created by enthusiasts. These days, arriving at Refdesk's well-organised page feels like a breath of fresh air. Created by Bob Drudge (father of notorious web reporter Matt Drudge, who broke the Monica Lewinsky scandal), this brilliant site aims to be the reference librarian of the web, and contains more than 20,000 links to reference sites. For an idea of its serious approach, have a look at the women's category: listings for Menopause Online, the International Center for Research on Women and much more.

### Research-It!                    www.itools.com/research-it
Once described as the Swiss Army knife of research instruments, the general appearance of this versatile site has stayed unaltered for years – an eternity in Internet time. It remains a beautifully simple place to begin any hunt for information. Search through various dictionaries and thesauruses, look up acronyms and quotations, translate English to French and back again, search the King James Version of the Bible and the works of Shakespeare, look at maps, check your stocks, and so on. You can do all these things better elsewhere, but no other site brings them all together quite like this.

### Resource Central                    www.resourcehelp.com
Oh dear. Oh good! This must be one of the worst designed, fiddly sites around, but because it has over 11,000 excellent links – listing useful resources, references, and research sites – it's worth perse-vering with. New links are added from a huge variety of sources and by user suggestions. Each category on the home page has a drop-down menu which takes you to more focused information – so 'Government' will give you further options that include 'elections', 'embassies' and 'United Nations'.

### Search.com                    www.search.com
The idea is that you only have to search once for results from over 700 search engines, directories, news sources, discussion groups and reference sites. You can use the site's specialised search channels to find information in specific areas. So clicking on Music brings up information related to MP3s, lyrics, reviews, prices, software and concert tickets. An uncomplicated introduction to search engines, but without any of the useful extras that they use to narrow your search.

**The Spire Project**          **www.spireproject.co.uk**

Tired of not finding what you want? This easy-to-use site opens up gated databases – those hard-to-find sites that charge you for access. Although there are many links to free information here, it's as a gateway to paying commercial databases, research services and document libraries that the site comes into its own.

## History of the Internet

*If you're really interested in the medium itself, try some of these sites.*

**Hobbes' Internet**          **www.isoc.org/guest/zakon/**
**Timeline**          **Internet/History/HIT.html**

This is an excellent hyperlinked history of the Internet.

**The Internet Society**          **www.isoc.org/internet-history**

Vint Cerf's Internet Society is an international organisation that supports Internet growth and develops and maintains Internet Standards. It has a good page of links to Internet histories.

**Net Timeline**          **www.pbs.org/internet/timeline**

If you find Hobbes' Timeline (above) a little complicated, try this excellent brief introduction from the US Public Broadcasting Service.

**World Wide Web Consortium**          **www.w3.org**

Chaired by Tim Berners-Lee and based at the Massachusetts Institute of Technology, W3C (as insiders call it) was created in October 1994 to develop common Internet protocols – the languages and procedures that keep the whole thing going. As you'd expect, the site is chock-full of information about the web – past, present and future.

**<w3history\>**          **www.w3history.org**

A genuinely accessible project and work in progress, whose ultimate goal is a comprehensive history of the Internet and the web.

# 2//SEARCH SECRETS

The Internet's growth as a huge and vigorous store of the world's information continues at an unprecedented rate. Forrester Research (**www.forrester.com**) estimates that 1.5 million pages are added to the net each day. According to a recent survey by the NEC Research Institute (**www.neci.nj.nec.com**) the World Wide Web contains more than one billion pages on approximately three million servers. Inktomi (**www.inktomi.com**), the company that provides the search technology for many leading engines, says this number doesn't include mirror sites (where the same material is found under different URLs) or duplicate pages. Add them in, and Inktomi estimate that the web is made up of at least four billion pages!

As we've seen, there isn't a centralised library or catalogue. Users have to rely on search technology – software that scours the Internet and attempts to categorise what it finds – to help find and sort through these vast piles of information. For most of this, this means going to a search engine, and it's no surprise that today's popular search engines are consistently ranked among the most visited sites on the web.

### The right search site

As the Internet has grown, a huge range of services have sprung up to help you find what you are looking for. When you type words in to the 'search' box on a site such as Excite (**www.excite.com**) or Yahoo! (**www.yahoo.com** or **www.yahoo.co.uk**), you are asking powerful tools to find information in a number of different ways. There are three main types of search sites:

- Search engines compile indexes of sites on the web which they consult to answer your query

- Directories store names and addresses of sites in rigidly organised categories, usually compiled manually

- Meta-searchers pass on your query to a selection of other sites and then amalgamate and display the results.

If you consult a search engine, it will try to match your query to its database and return a list of sites that it believes correspond to your interests. Consult a directory, and you have slightly more control. Searching will produce a category or set of categories to choose from, or you can 'drill down' through the directory, using your own judgement to find a likely-looking category. If you are looking for an exact piece of information or a particular site, search engines are probably a better bet. Use directories when you have a general research subject in mind.

### How do search sites search?

Search engines typically consist of three major components. These are:

- **A search agent** – a piece of software (also known as a spider or crawler) that continually roams the Internet looking for new or updated web pages.

- **An index or catalogue** that stores the results of the spider's search. This index contains a copy of every web page the spider has visited. The index is regularly updated by the spider.

- **Powerful software** that takes requests for information, searches through the entire index for matches and produces pages of returns, ranked in order of relevance. The entire process takes a matter of seconds.

It might seem like search engines hunt the web, but what they are actually doing is searching through their own stored indexes for matches.

Because they all have different search and presentation packages, each search engine will produce different returns.

### How spiders crawl around the web

Contrary to their name, spiders do not move between sites collecting goodies which they bring back to the search directory. In fact, all search agents simply request pages from different websites, just as your browser does when you are surfing the net.

Each spider uses different strategies. In general they start with a historical list of URLs, particularly documents with many links elsewhere, such as server lists, 'What's New' pages, links pages and the most popular sites on the web. The spider scours these documents of links which it can then inspect.

Most search engines also allow people to submit URLs for inspection manually, so the spider knows it should check whether it has been indexed. When new sites go live, one of the most important things is to inform the search engines.

From these starting points the spider selects sites to visit and index. The way sites are stored depends on the spider: Some index all the HTML tags – commands inserted in the document that specify how the page should be formatted – or the first few paragraphs of text. Others attempt to analyse the HTML and index the entire document. Some simply look at a site's title, others search every page. Some simply record the metatags – special keywords, invisible to the viewer, programmed into the website to tell the search engines what is on the page. A furniture store in Dublin, for example, might make use of metatags such as 'table' 'chair' 'futon' 'Dublin' 'shopping' and so on.

The software doesn't actually *know* what's on the page. Computers cannot tell what information on a web page is relevant and what isn't. So each search engine assesses the relevance of its indexed sites to your query using artificial criteria.

### Ranking for relevance

Most search engines return results with relevancy rankings. These list the returns according to how closely the search engine thinks they match your query. You'll often find yourself baffled by high-scoring pages that appear to contain completely irrelevant results.

This is because each search engine has different ways to assess relevance. Some will rank references according to where they fall in the document, so that a web page returning a match in the first few paragraphs is deemed more relevant than a page with references later on. Others ask how many times it can make a reasonable match within the same document. Some put the most popular sites (ranked by number of visits, or number of links to the site from other sites) first. Others use cunning tricks to try and ensure a better match, using a separate database of related terms so that if (for example) you are looking for 'spring water', a document with the words 'mineral water' or 'spa' would rank higher than one which contained the words 'spring break' or 'hot water'.

Search engines tend to concentrate on the 'keyword' and 'description' tags inserted into the HTML code that makes up a web page. Some search engines will improve a site's rating if keywords are also contained in the text of the page, the title and the description, and most search engines use keyword frequency as their main way of determining whether a site is relevant.

So if you're researching the movie Casablanca and the word 'Casablanca' appears many times on a page, in general any page that repeats the word 'Casablanca' dozens of times has a better chance of returning at the top of the list, simply because the search engine thinks the page may contain useful information. The site might, however, actually be about Morocco's biggest city. In this case, you would need to refine your search (see below).

**Metatag trickery**
Many search engines index sites by so-called metatags. As we have seen, these are special keywords embedded by web developers and programmers in the documents' HTML code designed specifically to tell search spiders what is on their sites. A well

planned set of metatags improve a site's chance of being picked-up significantly. The site's designer therefore has some influence over which keywords are used to index the site, and can even write the description of the document that appears when it is displayed as a search engine return.

Some designers misuse this facility to draw users to their sites, and the net's pornographers are among the worst culprits. For example, a recent ploy has been to put the words 'Britney Spears' (one of the most popular searches on the web – no, we don't know why either) into keyword metatags, in the hope of luring searchers. The search engines devise various methods to circumvent this misuse, excluding sites they detect trying to trick them into higher listings.

When pages are spidered by the search engines, keywords can be weighted and indexed according to how high they rate against other pages using the same keywords. The search engines consider placement of keywords throughout the page and the context in which they are used. Sites can control how their page is indexed by using the meta tag to specify additional keywords to index, and a short abstract.

All this helps to explain why the same search submitted to different sites will produce wildly different results. Indeed, for tools designed to facilitate the easy discovery of information, search engines are surprisingly hit-and-miss. Relevancy rankings are a good way to judge search engines. You won't have time to explore hundreds of returns to determine which links are worth a further look. The more obviously relevant the results are, the more you'll return to that particular search engine.

However, you can get more relevant results from any search site simply by asking the right question – and refining your query using a range of simple techniques. Whatever search site you use, read the search tips it provides. They're there to help you get the most out of the site.

## Structure your query

You need to strike a balance between making your search too broad and too specific. While a poorly constructed query can result in millions of useless pages, one that is overly precise might mean that you miss sites that would have been of interest.

Search sites look first for the first word you key in, and then move on to later terms or keywords. Always prioritise your query by putting the most unusual or important term first. If you are checking on who was in Scorsese's movie *The Godfather*, enter Scorsese Godfather rather than Cast Godfather Martin Scorsese. It also helps to enclose phrases or proper names inside quotation marks. So: 'Martin Scorsese' and 'Godfather Trilogy'.

### Be specific

The biggest problem you will encounter when searching is coping with huge numbers of undifferentiated or indistinguishable returns. To counter this, try and tell the search engine as much as you can. The more you narrow your search, the more likely it is that you will get a precision result (but the more likely it is that you'll find nothing). If you like Asian cooking try 'indonesian wok recipes' rather than 'recipes.' If you are looking for specific information on the bugs in Office 2000, you will have more joy searching for 'Office 2000 bugs' than just entering 'Microsoft Office' into a search engine.

### Keyword searching

This is the most common way of searching the Internet. Most major search engines search their indexes by keyword. These should be supplied by the webmaster, but if not, it's up to the search engine to determine them. This means search engines select the index words they believe to be most important. They tend to give more weight to words at the top of the page, and to words that are frequently repeated.

Some search engines index every word on every page of the site. Others index only part of a page – for instance, Lycos (www.lycos.com) indexes the title, headings, subheadings and links to other sites, plus the first twenty lines of text and the 100 words that occur most. Go (www.go.com) picks up every word in the text except commonly occurring words such as 'a,' 'an,' 'the,' and 'is.' HotBot (www.hotbot.com) also ignores common words, while Altavista (www.altavista.com) claims to index every single word, even the most common ones.

Many search engines have trouble with stemming – words that appear within other words. As a result, keyword searches fail to distinguish between parts of words spelt the same way, but with different meanings (for example, soft furnishings, software and softeners). This is one of the biggest causes of irrelevant returns.

### Concept-based searching
This type of search attempts to determine what you mean, not just what you say. In an ideal world a concept-based search returns hits on documents covering the subject that you are researching, even if the words in the document don't precisely match the words you enter in the search engine. This type of search is based on a technique known as cluster technology, which relies on sophisticated linguistic and artificial intelligence theory. Excite (www.excite.com) is the most widely known search engine relying on concept-based searching at present, and newcomer Kenjin (www.kenjin.com) also uses this approach.

At present, this idea works better in theory than in practice. Concept-based indexing is a great idea, but it's far from perfect. The results are best when you enter a lot of words, all of which roughly refer to the concept you're seeking information about.

### Advanced searches
Most sites offer two different types of searches: standard and advanced. In a standard search, you simply enter a keyword and

click search. Advanced search options vary from one search engine to another, but often include the ability to search for more than one word, to give more weight to one term than the other, and to exclude words that may confuse results. You might also be able to search for words that are found near to other search terms. Some search engines even let you specify whether you wish to restrict your search to certain parts of web documents – for example the title or URL. You can usually find excellent guidance and tutorials on advanced searching on the search site. Read it, and experiment.

Some sites will only search for words or phrases, but most give you the opportunity to keywords combines with 'modifiers' or 'Boolean logic' to eliminate ambiguity and pinpoint information.

### Modifiers

Modifiers are symbols that instruct the search engine to do something specific with the word or phrase that immediately follows the symbol. Use modifiers when you want to find web pages that have one word on them but not another. Say you want information on Tony Blair but not on his baby Leo. You would ask the search engine for blair -leo. Most search engines support the three major modifiers. These are:

**+** Instructs the search engine to include the subsequent word. Use the + modifier when it is vital that a word must be included in your return. For example, searching for +cruise +kidman will return pages about Hollywood's golden couple (although you could also get some matches for a company called Kidman Cruises). All returns must include both words, although the order doesn't matter.

**-** Instructs the search engine to exclude the subsequent word. Use the - modifier when it is vital that a word must not be included in your return. For example, searching for morecambe -wise will return pages on the English seaside resort Morecambe (and maybe the comedian Eric Morecambe), but not any pages featuring wise men, owls or the funnyman's partner Ernie Wise.

**'** Putting the phrase in quotes instructs the search engine to search for the exact phrase within the quotation marks. Use the ' modifier when you want the exact phrase in the exact order. For example, searching for 'Morecambe and Wise' will only return pages relating to Britain's favourite comedy duo – you've asked for all the words, as they appear between the quotation marks.

**Boolean operators**

Although modifiers can be very useful, they are a fairly rigid way of tightening up your search query. A more flexible series of advanced search commands is to use 'Boolean operators' – special modifiers based on Boolean logic, a kind of algebra invented by the 19th-century English mathematician George Boole, who devised a method of defining mathematical values as either 'true' or 'false'. The system is widely used by computer programmers, so it is no surprise to find that it is a powerful and versatile way to put some punch into your searches.

Most search sites will let you use Boolean operators, although some (including Altavista and Lycos) only allow you to use these parameters on the advanced search page. The major Boolean operators, which you can insert between any number of keywords, are:

**AND** Instructs the search engine to find both entered words. So searching for Fred AND Ginger will return pages mentioning Fred Astaire and Ginger Rogers as well as pages mentioning Fred Flintstone and Ginger Beer, but not pages that only mention one of the two keywords. (If you want to find the words in order, use the quotation modifier outlined above, thus: 'Fred and Ginger').

**OR** Instructs the search engine to find either of the entered words. So searching for Fred OR Ginger will return pages about men named Fred or women named Ginger (or even men named Ginger, or the spice ginger). By using an OR search you are telling the search site that either Fred or Ginger will do: you're not looking for both.

**NOT** Instructs the search engine to exclude the subsequent word. So searching for Fred NOT Ginger will return pages about Fred (Flintstone, Astaire, etc) but none about Ginger Spice because you have deliberately excluded Ginger from your results.

## //ADDRESS BOOK

### Checking up on the search engines

*If you plan to take Internet research seriously, you're going to have to keep up to date with the latest search engine developments. Here's where.*

**ResearchBuzz**                    www.researchbuzz.com
Frequent updates on search engines, browser technology and web directories.

**Search Engine Showdown**    www.searchengineshowdown.com
Compare the size, overlap, unique hits, changes over time, and dead links of the largest web search engines. Compare power search features and capabilities. Then use the one you always use, probably.

**Search Engine Watch**                www.searchenginewatch.com
Helps you find all the major search engines, meta-search engines and kid-safe services. Provides extensive information on how to get the best out of search engines. Sign up for an informative monthly email.

**Search IQ**                        www.searchiq.com
Regularly visits each of the major search engines, directories and meta-search engines, ranking and evaluating their performances using a variety of terms from specific to general. The differences are surprising.

**Traffick.com**                        www.traffick.com
Quirky source of news about portals – you know, those sites put up by ISPs and others to act as a first base from which to jump off into

the unknown. This site analyses the world of portals, aiming to 'help enhance your web experience' by helping you keep on top of their ever changing options. How nice.

| **Web Search from** | **http://websearch.about.com/** |
|---|---|
| **About.com** | **internet/websearch** |

Providing an extensive collection of quality web search links, this site will help you build your own arsenal of web search strategies and techniques. Aims to get you thinking like a 'power searcher' – whatever that is – in no time.

---

### Search sites

---

*See the directory chapters for extended analysis of the best sites to research particular subjects, but here's the lowdown on general search sites.*

*Everyone has their own favourite search site, but at the time of going to press many commentators believed that Google (www.google.com) and Yahoo! (www.yahoo.com) were head and shoulders above the rest. Try to become familiar with at least two or three others, so you have options if your favourite does not produce the required result. Take a look at each engine's advanced search options. This will save you time in the long run, and make it easier to work out which engine best suits your needs.*

### The best

---

**Google**  www.google.com

By consistently giving its users accurate, highly relevant search results, Google has won a deserved reputation as an incredibly powerful search engine. A technology double-award winner in the millennial Webby Awards (the Internet equivalent of the Oscars), Google's appeal lies in the quality of its results and its uncluttered homepage, which has no adverts, news headlines or categories to confuse things.

Google has sprinted into the leading position as the web's largest search engine by introducing the first billion-plus page directory index. According to Google, this also contains the largest collection of international sites on the Internet. Although other search engines previously claimed to have identified more than a billion pages, Google is the first to let searchers actually see them.

Due to its sophisticated link analysis, Google returns the most popular sites at the top. Link analysis technology ranks every website's importance based on what other sites link to it. Google looks at what other sites on the web have found useful enough to link to and return those pages first. This means that if the best match is an obscure site hiding away in some under-visited corner of the web, Google might miss it. Google's reasoned argument is that if it's so good, how come no one is using it?

Google only searches for pages that exactly match your search terms, so if you don't find what you're looking for first time, try different terms. Unlike most other engines, Google automatically adds the Boolean operator AND between the words you enter and only returns pages that include all your search terms – so the more terms you use, the more focused your search. If your search seems in the right area but is still giving too many results, it's easy to try a new search that only looks within the URLs returned by your first query.

So confident is Google that it can return exactly what you are looking for that its I'm Feeling Lucky button gives you the chance to go directly to the top-ranking match for your query – you won't even see the other search results. While this works extremely well if you are looking for something obvious like an institution or a company homepage, most of the time it is worth seeing what else Google returns in case you are looking for something a little bit different.

The GoogleScout option lets you search the web for pages that are related to your result. Click the Similar Pages link and Google will find about a dozen good quality matches. For example, using GoogleScout on a company's page will often show that company's competitors. From the result page you can also click on the Show matches link, which will show the cached contents of the web page at the time Google indexed it. Google is the only search engine to store web pages in its cache for users to use as back-up if the page they want to consult is temporarily unavailable.

## The rest

### All the Web                          www.alltheweb.com

Until Google announced its billion page index, 'All the Web, All the Time' seemed an almost fitting trademark for Norwegian company FAST's search engine. According to a recent report, by mid-1999, the web contained more than 800 million documents. Using their FAST Web Crawler, All the Web claim to have discovered that more than half these documents are duplicates. In May 1999, FAST launched with a catalogue size of 80 million documents. The site now claims to have indexed more than 300 million.

Although its bold claim to index the entire web now looks a little foolish, All the Web is certainly one of the fastest and most accurate search engines available, returning relevant results from even the most general of requests. There is still some way to go before the site lives up to its name, but the inclusion of many foreign language returns – in 25 different languages – is a positive sign. As well as the basic search, the site lets you search more than 17 million pictures and at least one million MP3 music files.

### Altavista                           www.altavista.com

Launched in 1995, Altavista was one of the first free search engine services. Attempting to use the latest technology to index every single word on the web, it was the most powerful search engine then invented. Backed by the enormous computational power of Digital, Altavista's brutal 'biggest is best' approach is a little primitive, but it works. Kind of.

It may no longer have the largest index of sites, but the service remains one of the most popular search engines around. This is surprising when Altavista is actually a rather poorly structured service that is probably the most disorganised – and consequently hard to use – of all the major sites. Altavista's major drawback is that it returns every page your search term appears in, so the simplest query can produce thousands of matches.

The Related Searches feature also reveals the underlying problems. After your search Altavista suggests what it thinks are related searches in the results box. Click on any of these links to launch a new search, using these new terms. Nine times out of ten this new search will take you further away from what you were originally looking for. There is a reasonable chance that you will find what you're looking for on Altavista, though it's something of a lottery.

One of the first search engines to offer foreign language searches, Altavista's Babelfish (at **http://babelfish.altavista.com**) makes a reasonable fist of translating any foreign language pages you may find.

**Ask Jeeves**                                   **www.ask.co.uk**
Offers a different approach to most search engines by making it possible to ask real questions in plain English. Jeeves responds by presenting a selection of closely related human-generated questions to which it knows the answer. That's the theory anyway. Ask Jeeves can answer logical and simple queries well and is a fun and appealing way to search. Moreover, it doesn't produce page after page of results. For this reason it's probably best for new users.

AskJeeves has become popular because it lets you ask your question the way you'd normally ask it, thus humanising the search process. The site's downside is that all too frequently, your question leaves Jeeves bemused, and you with a useless results page.

Imagine you want to find out the population of Scotland. With most search engines your query would look like this: population AND scotland. Jeeves lets you submit your question like this: 'How many people live in Scotland?' The site then supplies a page of what it hopes are similar questions to which it knows the answer – in this case, Where can I find official census data for the United Kingdom? and a link to the Government Statistical Service.

## Excite                           www.excite.co.uk or www.excite.com

Despite its rather modest index, Excite is one of the most popular engines on the web. What makes Excite worth a try is its 'Intelligent Concept Extraction' (ICE) technology. A conceptual rather than keyword-based way of searching, ICE is a type of artificial intelligence that attempts to understand what you are looking for.

When checking your search query against its index, Excite calculates the frequency with which certain important words appear. The theory is that when several words or phrases that signal a particular concept appear close to each other in a text, the search engine concludes that the piece is about a certain subject. Excite has a useful 'Search for more documents like this one' which you can use when a particular page returned is near perfect and you want similar information.

Because of ICE, results on Excite are often different to those on other engines. For example, when you look for 'young people', Excite will also bring up sites that focus on youth and children because it recognises that these are different ways of expressing the same concept.

## GO Network                                          www.go.com

Despite new owner Disney's best efforts to make GO (formerly Infoseek) indistinguishable from its competitors, there are still some useful search options lurking within. Providing consistent quality results, particularly in response to broad queries, Infoseek was deservedly popular. But things have moved on, and the Disney

Corporation does not appear to have put much thought into improving the search tools bequeathed to it.

One interesting option is the pipe (|) – on most keyboards you'll find this symbol just to the left of the space bar – which lets you simultaneously conduct a narrow search within a broader one. If you are looking for information on bagpipes within the bigger category of musical instruments your search would look like this: bagpipes|instruments. It works well, though it's hard to imagine it becoming a regular part of your search routine.

Go also lets you search within results, which is a useful feature when your first search is in the right direction but just a little too general. If Go finds you a page you like you can ask for more of the same by clicking on find similar pages. The Goguardian filter, which screens undesirable content, makes this a safe place for your kids to search the web.

### HotBot                                            www.HotBot.com
Part of the Wired group of sites (so ultimately owned by Lycos), HotBot returns accurate results that many users describe as 'smarter' than other engines. HotBot is coy about the exact science behind their ranking criteria, and on paper it doesn't look much different from their competitors, but it often produces superior returns. The site is well used by researchers, drawn by the variety of useful power-searching features – and above all, its ease of use. HotBot lets you build sophisticated search queries using simple pull-down menus, and allows you to ask questions in plain English.

A useful menu on the left-hand side of the main page helps users to fine-tune their search. You can also search by date – thus eliminating irrelevantly timed sites if you are searching for a specific news story. The site has a pleasingly simple interface where searching is obviously a priority – so it's sad, or annoying, and sometimes both, that results are preceded by adverts for related books or music.

## Kenjin                                    www.kenjin.com

Launched earlier this year by British-based search specialists Autonomy, Kenjin is a downloadable piece of search software that takes account of context when it searches. Instead of going out to an Internet search site, Kenjin sits on your PC (unfortunately there is no Mac version as we went to press).

Via a little window at the bottom of your screen, Kenjin automatically suggests links to related content as you read or type text within any Windows application. By bringing information to you automatically, Kenjin hope to eliminate the need to stop and search. The theory is that it examines the concepts, not keywords in your active window and consequently delivers links to more relevant information – but at present Kenjin seems to be speaking a different language.

Anyone annoyed by little pop-up windows (Help, anyone?) will find Kenjin a little intrusive, and at present the concept is still in its infancy. At the moment, Autonomy's promise that Kenjin actually learns how you search as you use it appears difficult to believe, but if it works this will be a radical addition to the researcher's armoury.

## Lycos                                    www.lycos.com

Initially a pure search engine, within the last year Lycos has switched tack and now styles itself more as a directory, following the model set by Yahoo. However, the search feature is still prominently displayed on the home page. To search Lycos, type your keywords into the search box and click Go Get It. Choose the Search These Results option if you want to tighten up your initial search. Lycos' best feature is its Popular sites option on your results page. These are excellent sites chosen by Lycos staff to match prevalent searches and lead you to what you're looking for.

Lycos ranks hits according to how many times your keywords appear in their indices of the document and in which fields they appear (i.e., in headers, titles or text). It also takes into consideration whether the documents that emerge as hits are frequently linked to other documents on the Web, reasoning that if other people consider them useful or interesting, you might too.

One aspect of the site that will keep you coming back to Lycos is its excellent MP3 finder at mp3.lycos.com. Lycos was the first major search engine to launch a specific MP3 search engine and it remains the market leader. Lycos have indexed more than one million tracks, with hundreds more added every day. There's more on MP3s on page 144.

**Northern Light**                               **www.northernlight.com**
A professional researcher's favourite, Northern Light is surprisingly little known, despite its huge index and excellent search and presentation options. Northern Light is named after a clipper ship built in Boston in 1851. She had a radical new design, and became known for her speed and groundbreaking technology.

Search results here are grouped into what Northern Light calls Custom Search Folders, which make looking for information easier by grouping results into meaningful categories. They are not pre-set like web directories, but are unique to each search.

These folders lead you to the exact results you want. For example, if you do a search on bond, you might receive more than a million results. As Northern Light doesn't know which meaning of bond interests you, it suggests a series of options for you to choose. These might include mutual funds, exchange rates and James Bond movies.

As well as the normal results, Northern Light holds a 'Special Collection' of documents, not available on other search engines, for which you have to pay a modest fee. These are held in an online library that combines more than 6,000 full-text journals, books, newspapers, magazines and reference sources. This is a unique range of information that includes such diverse sources as *The Lancet* and PA Newswire.

Most of these sources include articles dating back to at least January 1995. Before you buy information from the Special Collection item you always receive a full summary of the article. Searching these documents is free, but you will be charged between $1 and $4 to view them. If you want accurate information from a respected source, it's well worth it.

## Directories

*Created by teams of individuals, directories are by nature selective. Only humans can instinctively understand a site's meaning and relevance, and can logically place it in the correct area. The advantage is that a good directory will bring order to the chaos of Internet information. The drawback is that the size of the directory is limited by the need for human labour.*

*Web directories categorise sites by topic. Clicking on a major topic will take you on to something more specific, and then on into subtopics until you find the precise categories of sites you are interested in. Come to a directory if you don't know the exact name for the thing you are looking for, or if you want to conduct general research in a particular field.*

## The best

### Yahoo!                                    www.yahoo.co.uk

With over 145 million visitors every month, Yahoo! is the most popular site on the net. This also obviously makes it the most popular of all the search sites listed here. Yahoo's major selling point over its competitors is that sites are selected by humans rather than spiders or crawlers.

Yahoo! isn't the most comprehensive site by a long way. The pure search engines already mentioned all index more than 100 million Internet pages. In contrast, Yahoo! currently indexes only 1.5 million sites, but the ones that are listed are of a much higher quality, and there are fewer duplicate pages than on any other site. Yahoo! has also got round this by teaming up with Google: if the subject you want isn't in its own directory, Yahoo! asks Google to look.

What makes Yahoo! so popular is that it's easy to use. With its rigid categories funnelling users to the specific area they are looking for, Yahoo! is by far the easiest site for searchers to understand. For most users this far outweighs any doubts about how comprehensive it might be. When you begin a search, your results show the categories that match your search. Keep clicking on these categories to narrow down your search until you get what you want. You will find that Yahoo's editors do a pretty good job of listing the best sites.

One of Yahoo's drawbacks is the way it has restyled as a fully-fledged web portal with its own content and services (such as pagers, email, calendars, virtual greetings cards and so on). Although this has seen the stock market valuation of the company soar, it makes using Yahoo! to search for information a more distracting business than in its early days.

The most important thing to grasp about Yahoo! is that it is not a search engine, but a directory par excellence – indeed the original directory whose remarkable success has spawned all the others. This makes Yahoo! the right place to go if you're searching for the best sites in a popular topic.

### The rest

**About.com**                                                   **www.about.com**
About.com is one of the best directories on the web, and we'll be referring to particular parts of it throughout this guide. Information here is grouped into more than 700 separate areas, each with an expert guide. These areas focus on particular topics, with websites picked by the guide, who also generates editorial content and oversees the topics chat boards. The guides keep their particular area up-to-date and highly relevant.

This human dimension gives the site a real advantage over its competitors. For basic background on thousands of topics, more often than not these guides will point you in the right direction. Use About.com as you would a normal directory, by browsing through the hierarchically structured categories, or search through all the guides from the homepage.

**The Britannica Internet Guide**　　　　　　**www.britannica.com**

This is an excellent but highly selective directory of websites. Britannica's editors strive to include only the best sites on their listings. They review each site and assign a rating from one to five stars, based on the content and presentation of the site. Very few websites are awarded five stars, so if you dig up a five-star site here you can be sure it's pretty good.

**The Global Online Directory**　　　　　　**www.god.co.uk**

The guys who run this site are looking for quality over quantity. G.O.D's most useful feature is the Global Search which lets users search for websites within particular geographic regions, narrowing down the information to creating a more accurate result – select your region of choice from the pull-down Find it in the menu beneath the search box. As the Internet inevitably moves away from its current US focus to become truly global, the need for localised services will increase exponentially. It's no coincidence that this international outlook comes from the only established search service set up outside the US.

**GO Network**　　　　　　**www.go.com**

Go's major selling point is its small but excellent human-compiled directory of websites. It differentiates itself from most of its competitors by attempting to assess each site, and gauge its usefulness with a handy three-star ranking system. Unfortunately the listed sites come with the briefest of descriptions: one star means the site is good, two means it is very good, while three stars are reserved for the best of the web. In practice, this is a rather simplistic way of determining a site's worth, which doesn't give you enough of an idea whether a site is good, bad or simply OK.

**Google Web Directory**                    **http://directory.google.com**
Google, our top search engine, also has an excellent directory service, which applies its link analysis system to this human selected section. While most other directories list sites alphabetically, Google ranks sites by the number of links made to them by other sites. You can use Google's search engine and then jump straight to the directory it by clicking one of the category matches that appears beneath the result.

**LookSmart**                              **www.looksmart.co.uk**
The largest UK specific directory available to date, with more than 60,000 editorially reviewed URLs indexed into more than 12,000 categories. Search results are good and the descriptions for each site are concise.

**Open Directory Project**                    **http://dmoz.org**
The Open Directory, which uses human volunteers to catalogue the Internet, has probably already achieved its goal of producing the most comprehensive directory available. More than 26,000 contributing editors have listed nearly two million individual sites. This information is collected here, and also made available to any site that wants to use it through an open licence arrangement. Like About.com, the Open Directory benefits from human input: the difference here is that its users are also its editors.

Search as normal by inputting your query or browsing through the categories. Your result page lists the best sites at the top and the rest in alphabetical order. You can become an editor yourself through a link at the bottom of the homepage.

**SearchBug.com**                          **www.searchbug.com**
Based on research into what people are mostly looking for, this site collects, refines and organises websites in the categories that

people search for most. It has a handy clickable list of the most popular searches to save you typing in what you are looking for.

## Metasearch engines

*Key in a simple request and because of their different spider technologies, all the search engines will produce widely different results. Metasearch engines do not have spiders or an index of web pages; they send your search terms to the databases of other search engines, and some even combine your results into a single list. The best results come from uncomplicated queries, so keep it simple.*

*Metasearch sites cover a lot of ground quickly, but they have their disadvantages. You can't take advantage of special or advanced features of individual search engines and you are limited to basic searches. And quantity in results does not necessarily equal quality.*

## The best

### Copernic                                    www.copernic.com

Brilliant metasearch engine that sits in your own computer. It simultaneously consults the best search engines, brings back relevant results with summaries and removes duplicate information and dead links. Copernic has many customisable features – notably the ability to call up the returns of previous searches – and lets you search within your results using Boolean operators. It is easy to download (free of charge) via the Internet and to install. For serious searching using a single metasearcher, Copernic is hard to beat.

### MetaCrawler                                 www.metacrawler.com

This wee beastie sends your queries to different services, organises results into a uniform format, ranks them by relevance and returns them to you. The list of results can be sorted in different ways, including by relevance and source – and more unusually, by locality, region, and organisation. Metacrawler can be customised by using the Power Search to specify which search engines to use. If you don't want to download Copernic, MetaCrawler is the best general purpose, online meta-search engine.

## The rest

### The Big Hub www.thebighub.com
Sending your search to ten separate sites, this engine provides users with a convenient, efficient search.

### Dogpile www.dogpile.com
One of the most popular meta-search sites, and you can customise it to send questions to your favourite search engines first. Results are retrieved in lists of ten hits from each engine queried, but frustratingly these are not aggregated into one list. It works well, but it's crammed full of advertisers trying to sell you something.

### Ixquick Metasearch www.ixquick.com
Ixquick brings the top ten results from each search engine, and aggregates the results. For those who like that kind of thing, it also uses and reports on how the pages are ranked in each site. Ixquick awards one star for each search engine that placed a site in its top ten; a site that appears in multiple top tens is likely to be pretty good!

### Mamma www.mamma.com
Whaddaya mean you no a-like a my search results? Styling itself as 'the mother of all search engines', Mamma searches ten sites simultaneously, and consolidates results into a single list, with all duplicates eliminated.

## Other useful search sites

*If all else fails, or if you want to try something a little different, you could try these.*

### Direct Hit www.directhit.com
Measures what links people are clicking on at major search services across the web (no, don't ask us how) – thus determining the most relevant sites for your request.

**EuroSeek**                              **www.euroseek.com**

Ah, the pan-European ideal in action. EuroSeek enables you to search in any of the major European languages. As you would imagine, it covers European topics especially well.

**Inktomi**                              **www.inktomi.com**

A leading supplier of search services to other search engines, Inktomi's 500 million-page index gives users access to one of the largest searchable database of web pages so far.

**Karnak**                              **www.karnak.com**

Construct your own personal library. Karnak helps you form highly focused search queries, then emails you further results.

**Oingo**                              **www.oingo.com**

Type in your search word and Oingo returns a series of possible meanings – a bit like a thesaurus. Use the drop-down menu to select the exact meaning of your search and Oingo!

**RealNames**                              **www.realnames.com**

The best place to find Coca-Cola or Ford. Many company sites have registered RealNames – specialised keywords designed to take you straight to the right site. Check here first, or chance your arm and type in the company name followed by '.com' – e.g., www. ford.com.

**Searchengine.com**                              **www.searchuk.com**

The pop-up Hotlist Window offers you a simple way to visit sites listed in your results without cluttering up your desktop or requiring you to perform navigational gymnastics.

**UK Plus**                              **www.ukplus.co.uk**

Focusing on British sites, this is a useful starting point, complete with reviews of websites from a British perspective.

## What people search for

*Ever wondered what the rest of the world is searching for?*
*Here's where to find out.*

**The Lycos 50**                                    http://50.lycos.com
The 50 most popular Lycos user searches of the week.

**Metaspy**                                         www.metaspy.com
Voyeurs: come here for a glimpse of some of the searches being
performed at this very moment.

**Peek Through the Keyhole**        www.askjeeves.com/docs/peek
What people are asking Jeeves right now. And you can bet it's not
'Have you seen my trousers?'

**Search Spy**                                      www.kanoodle.com/spy
Interesting, but contains unfiltered content some people may
consider offensive.

**Word Tracker**                                    www.wordtracker.com
Discover the right keywords, and you'll see your website traffic
skyrocket. This is the place to find out how.

# 3//HELPING HANDS

The web is just one part of the Internet experience, and while it might seem like an endless treasury of information, it is in fact limited to the number of documents that people and organisations are prepared (or can afford) to make available. As a global communications system, the Internet also enables you to contact other people anywhere in the world who might be able to help, and for many people this is the most important aspect of the Internet.

This part of the online world is made up of three main sources:

**Usenet newsgroups** – electronic meeting places for groups of people with similar interests

**Mailing lists** – discussion groups that use email to exchange ideas and information

**Expert advice** – people with expertise in various subjects who offer their services, usually for free. These experts are usually reached via a website, but will then correspond directly with you via email.

Newsgroups and mailing lists are especially useful for the researcher, in that they address very specific subjects. Whether they are talking about nuclear physics or herbaceous borders, you will find knowledgeable and opinionated individuals in heated debate. The joy of these discussions is that providing they follow the basic rules, anyone and everyone can join in – whether they're the leading experts in a subject, amateur hobbyists or humble researchers looking for answers.

Unlike websites, with their fixed content and mainly commercial aspirations, newsgroups and mailing lists are open and democratic forums for debate. You'll find other users are usually only too happy to help you find what you are looking for, if only because it gives them a chance to show off what they know. Their uncensored, free-form discussions can be exhilarating – but there is no guarantee that the information in them is accurate.

### Newsgroups

The newsgroups are a pleasant hangover from the days before the World Wide Web. Entirely text-based, the newsgroups remain vibrant, defiant bastions against the commercialisation of cyber-space – and are still essentially true to their origins as academic debating grounds. They are now accessible through the web, but they're better used with a dedicated Newsreading program, such as the ubiquitous Outlook Express. All major browsers, including those from Microsoft and Netscape, also have newsreader programs.

Just as the web uses HTML and HTTP, newsgroups use an Internet language called Network News Transfer Protocol (NNTP). This enables anyone with a PC, an Internet connection and the right software to send a message to a news server – a dedicated computer that sends, receives and stores articles. ISPs all over the world run news servers for their subscribers to get articles and contribute (or 'post') their own. What's more – and here we approach the essence of Usenet, the collective name for all the newsgroups – every news server exchanges its articles with other news servers. Each ISP has its own news feeder that stores most Usenet postings from the last couple of days. The ISPs regularly update their list of postings, swapping data with other ISPs to ensure all versions are the same. This simple procedure passes messages and contributions around the globe.

There are more than 60,000 groups, with each newsgroup dedicated to a specific topic – covering everything from arthritis to Zen Buddhism and alcohol to UFOs. Each newsgroup has a unique name to help you identify what it's all about. Your newsreader should supply a list of newsgroups carried by your ISP, and if you want to read the articles, or 'subscribe' to a newsgroup, the procedure is simple. Users can post to existing newsgroups, respond to previous posts, and even create their own newsgroups.

## How Usenet is structured

Although there are tens of thousands of newsgroups, many are moribund or full of tedious in-jokes. Few ISPs carry more than 15,000 groups, which most people find is more than enough; you can always ask your ISP to add a newsgroup if you need it.

Newsgroups are arranged into subject hierarchies, with the first few letters of the newsgroup name indicating the major subject category and sub-categories represented by additional subtopic names, separated by a dot. Music lovers might subscribe to **alt.music** for freewheeling discussions and news; but fans of musician and DJ Moby will find specific news about the great man at **alt.music.moby**. Many subjects have several levels of subtopics.

The major hierarchies are:

**alt** – alternative topics (some say it stands for anarchists, lunatics and terrorists). Anything-goes type discussions covering every conceivable topic from aliens to Zen. For example, **alt.hemp** – rambling discussions by sundry dopeheads.

**biz** – business topics. Discussions about business products and services, including product debuts, upgrades, enhancements and reviews. For example, **biz.control** – be your own boss.

**comp** – computer-related topics. Discussions about hardware, software, languages, systems, and so on. Also a good area to tap into valuable consumer advice. For example, **comp.arch** – for coding freaks.

**humanities** – culture-related topics. Literature, fine arts and other humanities, for both professionals and amateurs. For example, **humanities.classics** – go Ancient Greek.

**misc** – miscellaneous topics. More serious than the alt hierarchy, misc covers employment, children, health and consumer issues ...

basically anything not covered elsewhere. For example, **misc.survivalism** – escape the city.

**news** – the Usenet itself. Information about the Usenet news network and software, including news servers and newsreaders. For example, **news.lists.misc** – important Usenet announcements.

**rec** – recreational topics. Discussions about arts, games, hobbies, music, sports, etc. If it's recreational, it's being talked about here. For example, **rec.humor** – lots of funnies.

**sci** – scientific topics. Pure- and applied-science discussions for both professionals and laymen. For example, **sci.space.shuttle** – keep in orbit.

**soc** – social topics. Social issues and cultures around the world, plus a place to socialise. For example, **soc.singles** – meet the (cyber) love of your life.

**talk** – general discussion. For example, **talk.religion.misc** – chat about churches.

In the original hierarchies, proposed new newsgroups must be nominated and voted on by other users before they are accepted. The alt hierarchy was specifically set up by people who wanted to discuss topics outside the remit of the standard hierarchies. Anyone can create an alt newsgroup, but some ISPs won't even carry the alt hierarchy because there are so many groups.

Some newsgroups are moderated, which means that all postings are read and reviewed for relevance and style before they go on the board. Most moderators are human volunteers, but some moderators are computer programs! One disadvantage of a moderated board is that postings to the group can be prevented from reaching users on the whims of one individual; another is that postings tend to take longer to appear, because they have to be vetted by busy people. However, moderated newsgroups have much less abusive slanging matches ('flames'), and are generally free of off-topic postings and spam.

## Where can I get more information?

New newsgroup users can find a helpful introduction at **news.announce.newusers** which has links to helpful information for new (and experienced) users of Usenet news, including information about test posting, spam, advertising, scams, FAQs, searching, how newsgroups work, identifying newsgroups of interest, creating new groups, and news reading software.

On the web, Deja News (**www.deja.com/usenet**) provides directories organised by subject that let you search and participate in the Usenet newsgroups.

One of the best ways to find groups is to use Remarq (**www.remarq.com**), which carries details of thousands of groups and mailing lists. While you can search postings through Deja, the major newsreaders only let you search through the names of the newsgroups. However, newsgroups are structured in a very organised way, so once you grasp the system, finding the right group becomes a lot easier.

## Newsgroup do's and don'ts

- Find out all you can about the group before actually joining. Many groups have a strong sense of community, with their own rules and traditions, and it pays to be polite on their patch.

- Read the postings for a while to make sure you're in the right place, and if the group has a list of FAQs read them too. You need to learn the conventions of the particular group before you speak up. The best way to do this is just to read (or 'lurk') for a couple of weeks, and see how the individual members act. You could also email a friendly-sounding individual in the group for tips.

- Post in the right place – don't post in alt.skincare when you should be in alt.food.chocolate.

- Don't ask things you could easily look up yourself.

- Don't ask for tutorials (look at the FAQs).

- Don't advertise or spam.

- Don't be rude or post in ALL CAPS – this is the Usenet equivalent of shouting.

- Remember that posting a message to a newsgroup doesn't guarantee a response. Don't be disheartened, try again – and check you're in the right group.

**Accessing the newsgroups**
*For more experienced Internet users, the most common way of reading the newsgroups is through the newsreaders – programs that download and organise messages stored at your ISP's news server – bundled free with major browsers. The most popular newsreaders are Outlook Express – which comes with Internet Explorer – and Netscape Messenger – which comes with Netscape Communicator.*

A major drawback of joining newsgroups and mailing lists is that marketers scour them for email addresses. You then get electronic junk mail, or spam, in your mailbox. One way to deal with spam is to post to newsgroups and join lists with a separate email address from the one you use for correspondence. A common ploy is to set up a free web-based email service like Hotmail (**www.hotmail.com**) and use that address; some of these services even have 'bulk mail' folders where they put multiple mailings, so you need never see them.

Most newsreaders let you download articles you're interested in, so that you can read them offline later. If you want to reply or post a message, the newsreader stores your instructions and activates them the next time you go online.

Subscribing to a newsgroup does not involve any sort of registration or joining process. It simply means that you've instructed your newsreader to check for new postings from that group every time you connect. You are still free to post and read messages from all other groups, whether or not you have subscribed to them. For any message, you can choose to reply directly to whoever posted it, or you can post a reply to the newsgroup.

To find information on a specific topic, try searching for words in the list of newsgroup titles, using the keyword search option in your newsreader. If this proves fruitless go to **www.deja. com/usenet**, which lets you search the entire Usenet for words and phrases. You can then subscribe to any newsgroup that matches your research needs.

**The major newsreader programs**
Microsoft's Outlook Express newsreader is probably the best newsreader around today. The interface is very practical, with separate panels showing news servers, article headers and the contents of your chosen message. Netscape Messenger is much the same, but Outlook Express works better offline, letting you read downloaded messages at your leisure, and has better filtering capabilities to help eliminate the dreaded spam.

Of the specialist newsgroup programs, three in particular stand out. Because you're paying for these you expect them to be good, and all three have particular features that set them apart from the competition. If you're planning to spend a lot of time researching the newsgroups then one of these programs is worth the investment.

**Gravity**                              **www.microplanet.com**
With lots of message-sorting options this flexible newsreader has a good reputation. You can read existing articles or subscribe to new groups while downloading, and there's a handy image browser. Best of all is the message rules feature, which lets you eliminate all

messages from any particularly annoying individuals, simply by dumping their address in the Bozo Bin. Costs $39.95.

### NewsMonger
www.techsmith.com

Offering some useful search facilities, this program is designed to help you locate messages of interest. After selecting the newsgroups to search, you specify keywords, and the program finds any matching messages. You can also set it up to perform automatic searches. Costs $39.95.

### Virtual Access
www.atlantic-coast.com/va

This program is particularly good at helping you organise your messages. If you're a heavy Usenet user it has excellent book-marking options which let you find important messages with ease. There are also powerful message filters that do a good job reducing spam. Costs $59.

---

**News about newsgroups**

Check out these groups for general information and updates on the newsgroups. They provide excellent starting points for general enquires, and tell you all you need to know about the way newsgroup addresses are structured.

**alt.config** – how to set up your own newsgroup.

**alt.culture.www** – developments in the web's infrastructure.

**alt.current-events.net-abuse** – stay up to date with spam.

**bit.listserv.new-list** – find out about new mailing lists.

**comp.internet.net-happenings** – see what's new on the Internet.

**news.announce.newsgroups** – see what's new on the Usenet.

**news.answers** – endless answers to your Usenet FAQs.

**news.groups.questions** – the Usenet help desk.

**news.lists** – find out how many newsgroups there are.

**news.newusers.questions** – good if you're new and having problems.

To find a newsgroup, you could simply search the list of all newsgroups that your newsreader downloads the first time you connect. In reality this is unrealistic: there will be a huge amount of them, and newsgroup names are often puzzling, so this method would be more than a little time-consuming.

### All about Deja.com

Anyone having trouble locating what they're looking for on the Usenet should turn to Deja.com (**www.deja.com/usenet**). A researcher's treasure, the site has recently attempted to reposition itself as a commercial product research site (you will find lots of useful product information here). Bypass the homepage and head for the Usenet section and you'll find this popular gateway remains by far the easiest way to search the newsgroups.

Deja is a vast site that allows you to easily search through virtually all the groups. Because you can search for specific words and phrases Deja is an excellent tool for anyone who wants to look through Usenet information but hasn't got hours to spend hunting through thousands of groups.

Deja holds a huge database of past messages in all the main areas. Usefully, you can search not just for particular words or phrases, but also for all messages by a particular individual.

### Deja's power search

Although it is easy to search on Deja's Usenet homepage – just enter what you are looking for in the query box and click search – the power search is a far more flexible way of finding exactly what you are looking for. Perhaps you're looking for clear, unbiased opinions on a new product for your business. A brief search reveals that a certain Helen Edwards seems a particularly authoritative commentator in this area. Using Deja's power search you can then search all her previous postings. Here's how it works:

Enter your query into the Enter Keywords search box. Indicate whether you wish to match all or any of the keywords entered. Deja will use this information to search both the name and the full text of the newsgroups.

Make sure the Results type is on discussions (Deja's term for the newsgroups) and take your pick of 18 languages – or select any.

If you want to limit your search to articles with particular words in their subject line, enter those words in the Subject box. If you know the name of the particular newsgroup you want to search, enter it in the Forum box. If you want to search all the articles posted by a particular individual, you must enter their email address in the Author box, and if you want to focus your search on or after a particular date, enter those dates in the Date boxes.

When you have entered all the information you wish, decide whether to display results by Confidence, Forum, Author or Date, choose how many results to display and hit Search.

Deja is one the most powerful and flexible search engines on the Internet, but it has some rather unusual ways of tightening up your searches. Try these symbols:

| Symbol | Action | Example |
|--------|--------|---------|
| * | Wildcard search for part of a word | ben* |
| ' ' | Search for a complete phrase | 'Ben Nevis' |
| & | Use like the AND modifier | ben & nevis |
| I | Use like the OR modifier | ben I nevis |
| &! | Use like the NOT modifier | ben &! nevis |

| ^ | Search for words near each other (within five characters) | ben ^ nevis |
| {} | Search newsgroups alphabetically (all groups between those specified) | {alt.aquaria comp.lang.java} |
| ~a | Search for posts by specified author | ~a helen@ edwards.com |
| ~g | Search in specified newsgroup | beautiful ~g alt.supermodels |
| ~s | Only search within posts | ~s psychology |
| ~dc | Only search on specified date (note the US format) | ~dc 1994/08/16 |

**Reading Deja articles**

One you've specified your criteria and submitted your search, Deja returns a list of matching posts. The returns include the date and subject of the post, the newsgroup in which it appears and the author. Click on the subject link to read the full text.

Once you've found an article of interest, there are some useful options:

- If you want to see all the current posts in the newsgroup click Forum

- View all posts in the current thread by clicking Thread

- See other messages in the thread by clicking Previous in Search or Next in Search

- Reply to the message (on the public Usenet) by clicking Post Reply

- Email the author directly by clicking on his or her name.

**Mailing lists**

Like newsgroups, mailing lists are communities of people discussing their favourite topics. The difference is that it all works using ordinary email programs. By sending an email to the list, you ensure a copy is emailed to everyone on the list. Just as many companies and organisations use mailing lists as a way to keep in touch with their customers, so people with shared interests can keep in touch with each other.

Some of the most popular mailing lists are what are known as announcement lists. These work in the same way as a printed newsletter – although they usually have a huge reach – upwards of 1000 subscribers. They work in only one direction, from the publisher of the list to the subscriber, and tend to be distributed on a regular basis – daily, weekly or monthly. Announcement lists alert subscribers to news, important information and details of forthcoming events.

The discussion lists, on the other hand, are more like a public forum, offering you the chance to ask questions, express opinions and share information with other subscribers. These in turn are divided into public lists which are open to anyone, and private lists limited to members of a certain company or organisation. Of the hundreds of thousands in existence, only about one in five are public.

As with newsgroups, there are moderated and unmoderated lists. In the former, messages are read and (sometimes) edited or deleted before they are sent to subscribers, to ensure content is relevant. In contrast, unmoderated lists let you post just about anything – no one monitors the content of the messages before they are sent to the other subscribers.

One of the drawbacks of mailing lists is the huge number of individual messages you receive if you subscribe to a particularly active list. Thankfully, many lists offer a bundled version. If you select this option you get lots of messages delivered periodically in one go, rather than drips and drabs each time someone posts to the list. Bundles are delivered once a day, or are sent out when the list reaches a specific number of messages.

**How to find the right list**
Sometimes you'll find information about lists on the web. If you've hit a relevant site, there could be details of a list. You could also email webmasters of well-run sites asking whether they use or know of any good mailing lists. Or if you find an appropriate newsgroup, ask there – after checking the groups FAQ, of course.

If those avenues fail, there are plenty of websites that help you search for mailing lists by title or subject, read a basic description of the group and obtain subscription instructions. One of the best is Liszt (**www.liszt.com**) – see this chapter's address book.

**How to subscribe**
You need an email program that can create multiple mailboxes, so that you can screen and sort your mail into those boxes. Both Outlook Express and Netscape Messenger do the job more than adequately. You'll also want to be able to sort messages by subject, date, and author, and it helps if you can search your mail by keyword. The search feature is vital if you ever want to be able to look back at particular messages.

Some groups have their own websites that explain how you can subscribe, but many don't. Most lists are maintained by mailing list managers – software that makes subscribing easy, then makes sure that you get all the emails you've asked for. Make sure you send your subscription request to the list's administrative address. If you mail it to the regular list address it will be sent to all the list subscribers, instead of signing you up. This will make a pretty bad first impression.

When you subscribe to a discussion group it will automatically send you basic information about the group, including how to post messages and how to unsubscribe. It is a good idea to save this message for future reference.

## How to post

The whole raison d'être of mailing lists is to discuss things, so after you've read the posts for a while, feel free to contribute. To reply to a message, you simply open it and choose your Reply To command. The message subject will automatically appear at the. top of the message (the header), and on most lists, your reply will be addressed to the whole list, not just to the person whose message you are replying to.

As with newsgroups, you will find your contributions are better received if you follow mailing list etiquette – spamming the whole list with a request for the URL of Yahoo! will not endear you to anyone. So here are the golden rules.

- After you subscribe, spend some time seeing how the list works before you reply to anything yourself.

- Always include a heading in the subject line of anything you post, so others can follow the discussion without having to open every email. Ensure your messages conform to the group style.

- Stay relevant. If you post random comments, the rest of the group are not going to be happy. If you post to a home improvement list, don't assume everyone wants to hear about the football game you went to last night.

- DON'T SHOUT. Keep the caps lock off. If you use all capital letters in your posts, people will angrily ask you to stop shouting.

- Don't Spam. On many lists, posting adverts or commercial blurbs will get you thrown out. Permanently.

- . When replying to existing messages, only include bits of the original post which are directly relevant.

## How to unsubscribe

If you don't want to get any more mail, instructions for unsubscribing are usually included in the welcome message sent when you first joined the list. If you've lost that message, check to see whether incoming messages carry instructions at the end. If all else fails, you can ask for the instructions. The usual procedure is to send an email to the list's administrative address with the words 'unsubscribe listname' in the body of the message.

## Ask an expert

If you can't find what you're looking for in a list or newsgroup, or if you are looking for a rather uncommon piece of information, it's a good idea to ask a real person – preferably an expert or someone very familiar with the subject you are researching. Some innovative websites are bringing together experts who are willing to answer your questions to the best of their (often considerable) ability. Most of these sites are based in the United States.

Experts will not write five-page essays on the behavioural characteristics of an angry rhinoceros – but they are usually more than happy to answer legitimate questions that might help with a project or satisfy your curiosity.

*See below for the sites.*

## //ADDRESS BOOK

---

### Newsgroups

---

*We've already had a detailed look at the mighty Deja (www.deja.com/usenet), but it's not the only option when it comes to searching for newsgroups. A number of other sites offer some valuable alternatives.*

## The best

### RemarQ                                    **www.remarq.com**

Providing access to one of the most complete source of Usenet discussions, with more than 30,000 groups and ruthless suppression of spam, RemarQ is a great place to find and read newsgroups. This site's beauty is its simplicity. Whilst it doesn't have quite as many search options as Deja, this is a genuinely easy place to access newsgroups with the minimum of fuss. Discussions are awarded stars – the more replies from different authors, the more stars. One of RemarQ's best features is the way it makes the Usenet easy to digest by renaming newsgroups for easy identification. For example, the Usenet name for one newsgroup about travel round Europe is rec.travel.europe. RemarQ calls the board 'European Travel' to make it easier for people to find and identify.

## The rest

### Cyberfinder                               **www.cyberfinder.com**

Browseable and searchable hierarchical subject listings of Usenet groups.

### Jammed                                    **www.jammed.com**

A good index of comprehensive Usenet FAQs.

### Newsguy                                   **www.newsguy.com**

The nicely organised service is an easy-to-use destination that gives its members access to more than 7,500 Usenet newsgroups. For a fee, you can join Extra Newsguy and get access to over 25,000. Newsgroups here are kept virtually spam-free by Spam Hippo, one of the best available anti-spam agents.

### NewzBot                                   **www.newzbot.com**

Most Usenet servers are properly configured to only allow connections from local users – and most Usenet servers carry o nly a selection of Usenet groups. This is where the NewzBot comes in. If you find out that there is a useful new group called

**alt.support.autism**, but your local news server doesn't carry it, use NewzBot to find – and access – a server that does.

## Mailing lists

### The best

#### Liszt                                                    www.liszt.com

Liszt is a huge directory of Internet discussion groups, including mailing lists, newsgroups, and chat channels: there are more than 90,000 mailing lists there. Before Liszt, nobody had ever attempted to gather all the mailing lists in the world together in one directory. The site is an endlessly useful way of finding groups on the Internet – whatever it is you need information on.

You wouldn't use Liszt to read or access mailing lists; the site just helps you to find lists that might be of interest, with a powerful search facility. Then it tells you how to get more information about the list, including details on how to join. Once you've found a mailing list you will still have to use your email program to join.

### The rest

#### ListTool                                                www.listtool.com

This is a free service that automates the process of subscribing, unsubscribing and sending commands to over 600 mailing and discussion lists from categories such as art, music, computers, news, and business.

#### RemarQ                                                  www.remarq.com

As well as its excellent newsgroup finder (see above), RemarQ also makes searching for mailing lists easy. To locate a specific list, enter the name or topic followed by the word mlists. If you want to find a list about Canada, for example, you would enter 'Canada mlists' in the search box. Items indicated with a key icon on your result page are mailing lists. RemarQ will send your subscription request to the list owner on your behalf, but if you want to stop receiving mails, you must notify the list owner yourself.

**Topica** www.topica.com

Nice design. Topica helps you easily find discussions and information on virtually any topic, from competitive giant marrow growers or Ally McBeal, to Java software groups and industry insider newsletters. The site combines an easy way to subscribe with one of the most comprehensive guides to discovering existing lists.

## Other useful sites

*A good way to find out whether there is a mailing list covering your particular interest is to search Vivian Neou's List of Lists (http:// catalog.com/vivian/interest-group-search.html) – one of the largest directories of special interest group mailing lists on the Internet. Also worth a look is http://paml.net – an up-to-date index of Publicly Accessible Mailing Lists arranged alphabetically by name and by subject. At www.tile.net, you can search lists by name, description or (and this is the useful bit) domain. This means you can find a list based in Britain, France or, for the real obscurantist, Western Samoa. You can also search Yahoo's mailing list discussion groups at (deep breath now) http://search.yahoo. com/bin/ search?p=mailing+lists – they are listed by subject category.*

## Ask the experts

### Allexperts.com www.allexperts.com

The site has thousands of volunteers, including top doctors, engineers, and scientists, waiting to answer your questions. All answers are free and most come within a day, and this is the only site to guarantee an answer within three days. This is a fast loading, simply designed, easy-to-use guide with pages that load nice and quickly.

### Ask a Librarian www.earl.org.uk/ask

Public libraries throughout the UK man this brilliant reference service. Whatever the subject of your enquiry, Earl's librarians can help. Ask a question on the enquiry page and it will be automatically routed to one of the participating libraries, where skilled reference librarians will identify the best source of information – print or electronic. They then send you an email with their findings.

### Askanexpert        www.askanexpert.com

This site lets you check the resumés of hundreds of people, from astronauts to zookeepers. When you've found the right expert, click the link to visit their site. If you can't find what you're looking for there, you're free to email the expert with your query.

### Ask-A-Question        www.ipl.org/ref/QUE

Although still at an experimental stage, this service from the exceptional Internet Public Library is a good place to get started with some ideas and places to begin if you have a big project to research. Specific questions get brief factual answers, but if you have a broader topic of interest, the librarians at the IPL will send you a short list of sources for further explanation.

### AskMe.com        www.askme.com

Volunteer 'experts' man this hugely professional, easily navigable destination rather than individuals screened by the site, so this one is best approached cautiously. From the home page you can browse through experts in particular categories – so if you're searching art history, you'll find experts in ancient art, renaissance art and modern art.

### AskTony        www.asktony.com

This British-based site employs skilled Internet researchers who use the net to find answers to your questions. Don't let the appalling design deter you. This is a popular service that delivers results, partly by prioritising questions that seem genuine. You wouldn't ask Tony a spoof question, would you?

### ExpertCentral.com        www.expertcentral.com

This site is so easy to navigate that even the most desperate technophobe will love it. There are 7,000 experts here to advise on topics as diverse as aerobics and palaeontology. Initially these clever folk will answer briefly for free. If you would like them to do more digging or to write a report, then they will propose a fee, which is usually negotiable.

**Information Outpost**                    **www.informationoutpost.com**
This free site's human researchers endeavour to send you a URL or two answering to your question within 24 hours. If they need more time to investigate at a library, they'll send a further email with the results.

**LookSmart Live**                          **http://live.looksmart.com**
An interactive site that brings members together to share their knowledge and find answers – which are rated by the questioner. An answer rated 'Very helpful' gets a score of three, 'Generally OK' gets a score of two and 'Didn't help me' scores one. This is a good way to judge how likely you are to receive a useful answer from the same expert. The site calculates contributors' overall averages and also works out the overall ratings for each category. Registration is free and easy.

**The Virtual Reference Desk**                          **www.vrd.org**
The AskA locator at the bottom of this sites home page takes you to an enormous list of expert sites organised by subject. There may be more than one site with the same name listed, but each link leads to an individual resource. The VRD does not actually answer questions, but provides links to experts who do.

---

### Specialist expert sites

---

**Ask a Geologist**                          **http://walrus.wr.usgs.gov**
The right place to ask questions about mountains, rocks, rivers and so on.

**Ask an Astronaut**                          **www.starport.com/live/astro**
Space-related questions answered by real-life astronauts. Don't ask

them whether man really did walk on the moon. They've probably heard it a thousand times.

**Ask Dr Universe**                    www.wsu.edu/DrUniverse
Why does electricity shock? Fun site (mainly for kids) that lets you question what appears to be the world's most knowledgeable cat.

**Ask Shamu**        www.seaworld.org/ask_shamu/asindex.html
Killer whales who know lots about marine biology and the environment. Crazy, crazy stuff.

**Ask Slashdot**                    http://slashdot.org/askslashdot
Detailed responses to any computer related question.

**Ask the Experts**                    www.sciam.com/askexpert
Why do we sneeze? Thousands of science queries answered.

**Expert Search**                    www.expertsearch.co.uk
Find experts in medical and industrial subjects. Could be the right place for those tricky pharmaceutical problems.

**Experts Exchange**                    www.experts-exchange.com
Answers to all your technology questions.

**net_query**                    www.bbc.co.uk/webwise/query
The ultra-reliable BBC gets brainy people to answer your questions about the Internet.

# 4//GENERAL DIRECTORY

So now you know the basics of how to track down those hard-to-find facts on the web, using newsgroups and on mailing lists. But this wouldn't be a Virgin Internet Guide without a comprehensive list of the most useful sites we could find.

Compiled alphabetically, this section covers every research angle we could think of – apart from education, business and genealogy, which are such big subjects that they deserve their own chapters.

You can search for names, addresses, phone numbers and email addresses; get financial advice and market information; find yourself a new job and sort out that computer problem; and teach yourself how to design your own website. Keep bang up-to-date with developments in the world of technology, tap into the enormous range of freely available music and pictures, dig through the world's most extensive news archives or give yourself a medical. If you're planning a trip overseas you can research the cheapest deal, get detailed maps and even learn the language. Or if you fancy it, you can save on the airfare and just travel virtually from your computer with insiders' travel guides that really show you what it's like.

Then there's a whole virtual reference library for you to browse. You can check your spelling at the world's most comprehensive dictionaries, verify facts at authoritative sites or get a range of free calculators to work out anything tricky for you. There are sites to help you research property and others to put your mind at rest if you have a pressing legal problem.

Enjoy!

## //ANTIQUES

*Collecting antiques combines a passion for beauty with a chance to learn about history. There are tips here about how to find, buy and look after just about anything. The following sites bring galleries, dealers and collectors together, and are among the best jumping off points to find out more.*

**About Antiques**                    http://antiques.about.com

A typically excellent About.com guide, this site covers a huge variety of topics, including fine porcelain and vintage accessories, with a professionalism and insider knowledge you'll come to appreciate. The 'how to' section explains topics like how to bid at auction, though it doesn't say how you should attract the auctioneer's attention.

**Antiques and Art Australia**          www.antique-art.com.au

Australia's best source of information for antiques, collectibles and antiquarian books. Among the extensive options are geographically arranged dealer and gallery listings broken down by dealer speciality. There's also a list of antique trade fairs and a handy 'ask the expert' service.

**Antiques**                        www.antiques-oronoco.com

A beautifully designed introduction, with useful information on all kinds of antiques and curios. The explanations are complemented by a lovely selection of images. There's also a refreshingly direct introduction to negotiating and bartering.

**The Antiques Directory**        www.antiques-directory.co.uk

Containing over 17,000 entries, this site helps you find dealers, auctioneers and restorers throughout the UK. With something going on almost every day of the year, the diary of antique fairs and flea markets is invaluable.

**The Antiques Roadshow**            www.bbc.co.uk/antiques

The UK's most popular antiques programme has a hugely impressive web presence. Particularly useful are the 'Tricks of the Trade' section, which explains how to look after your treasures, and the series of specialist guides – which provide succinct and helpful histories of different areas of interest written by Roadshow experts.

### The Antiques Trade Gazette    www.atg-online.com

The leading trade rag offers extensive coverage of the international art and antiques trade, including fair and auction calendars plus the inside news on markets and antiques centres. Informed market analysis makes this an essential bookmark for dealers and collectors.

### Antiques UK    www.antiques-uk.co.uk

Bigger than the deceptive homepage suggests, this site has much to offer, particularly for anyone researching an overseas purchase. There's a good selection of stock, with over 20,000 individual photographs of items for sale. Too much white text, however, makes the Worldwide Directory of Antique Dealers difficult to read.

### Antiques World UK    www.antiquesworld.co.uk

This easy-to-use site acts as forum for buyers, sellers and collectors, and also provides a very useful review section that recommends the best reference books in 48 specialist areas. There's also a comprehensive directory of trade, professional and research organisations, and contact details for collectors clubs.

### icollector    www.icollector.com

An e-commerce site and an excellent resource for researching art, antiques, and collectibles, this is a nicely designed site aimed at the knowledgeable enthusiast. There's a vibrant community area, the usual detailed events diary and links to associations online.

### World Collectors Net    www.worldcollectorsnet.com

This is a popular online meeting place for collectors. You will find information and features on dozens of popular collectibles, from precious Lomonosov porcelain to My Little Pony – plus free interactive message boards and an informative online magazine.

---

### Newsgroups

---

**rec.antiques** – discussing antiques and vintage terms

**rec.antiques.marketplace** – buying, selling and trading

# //AREA INFORMATION

*Before the Internet, looking up a business meant looking through a telephone directory, and if you wanted details on anywhere outside your immediate location, you had to trek to the local library. Now the Internet has established itself as the source of local information par excellence, and it's just as easy to find out about John O'Groats as Lands End, or to research Cape Town and California.*

**Big Book**                                    **www.bigbook.com**
Business information for over eleven million companies across Canada and the US, including maps and driving directions. If you want to shop, the site has easy-to-use local shopping guides with links to local yellow pages and city guides.

**Citysearch.com**                              **www.citysearch.com**
America's foremost local information provider. Whether you want to see a movie, book a table, reserve a room, buy a ticket or catch a show, you can do it online here. You can search by city or by zip code.

**COUNTYweb**                                   **www.countyweb.co.uk**
Useful business directory network that lets you examine details of the UK's top businesses. As well as providing up-to-date local news headlines and weather forecasting, the site helps you to research property, jobs and events on a regional basis.

**The Good Guide to Britain**                   **www.goodguides.com**
The site for the best-selling *Good Guide to Britain* and *Good Pub Guide* books. These searchable pages conveniently present all the information and recommendations from the latest editions, augmented by a calendar of events and some enticing itineraries.

**Information Britain**                          **www.information-britain.co.uk**
Cheesily showcases accommodation to suit every budget and a broad range of suggested places to visit. It's hard to agree with the site's assertion that the whole of Britain is one big film set, but

there are some surprises – did you know that parts of Lawrence in Arabia were filmed in the sand dunes of Merthyn Manor, South Wales? So much for the romance of the desert.

**Knowhere: A Users Guide to Britain**  www.knowhere.co.uk
This is a guide to more than a thousand UK towns and cities, compiled by people who actually live there. You'll find details on clubs, pubs and information about gigs, festivals and other events, shops and a candid, nay blunt, guide to the best and worst things about the place.

**PhoneNetUK**  www.bt.com/phonenetuk
Online version of the 192 telephone directory service – without the charge. Details are only displayed if the number appears in the printed phone book. The site holds number information for both People and Businesses, and it helps if you know some address details.

**Postcode Finder**  www.royalmail.co.uk/paf
Use this site to find any postcode in the UK – just enter address details and the site does the rest. If you do not know the address, but you have the postcode, the Address Finder can help. You are limited to 50 correct look-ups in any 24-hour period.

**Scoot**  www.scoot.co.uk
There's a special name for sites like this: infomediary. What that means is that they are middlemen between producers of goods and services and their potential customers. This highly innovative service is one of the best, covering 27,000 British villages, towns and cities. The People Finder is particularly useful for tracking down long lost friends.

**Telephone directories on the web**  www.teldir.com/eng
The most complete index of online phone books, with over 350 links to yellow pages, white pages, business directories, email addresses and fax listings from over 150 countries around the world. Only directories that make some attempt to be complete (preferably official ones) are included.

**ThomWeb Business Finder**  www.infospace.com/uk.thomw
With easy access to over 2 million UK business listings on the Thomson Directories database, this is a good place to find what you need quickly. You can access and search the database by name, classification or heading.

**TownPages**  www.townpages.co.uk
After one of the most dramatic introduction sequences of any website comes to an end, this site reveals itself as a useful service that caters for all local community needs.

**UK Telephone**  http://warwick.ac.uk/cgi-bin-
**Code Locator**  phones/nng
Takes telephone numbers, exchange names or the name of a location – and returns background about the area, a map location, BT charge details and the names of nearby exchanges. Good stuff.

**UpMyStreet**  www.upmystreet.com
You could spend hours messing around in here. It's a brilliantly simple service that lets you compare statistical data for two different areas. After entering your postcode the site draws a graph that plots house prices over the last five years, compared with any other area you please. You can also find out about council tax bands, crime rates, local services and much more.

**Yellow Pages**  www.yell.co.uk
Drawing from the same information as the paper directories – and using the same principles of ease of use and comprehensiveness – this site lets you search throughout the UK, the equivalent of 75 different paper directories.

## //ART & ARCHITECTURE

*Whether it's finding out about your favourite artist, hunting down a painting for your house or planning a weekend of culture, the Internet comes up trumps. You can browse the collections of the major museums in the world from the comfort of your desktop.*

*Simply key the museum into a search engine and you're off. Here are some other suggestions for cultural browsing.*

## The Art Connection      www.art-connection.com

A useful but drab site, which lets you search galleries for works by particular artists or on specific subjects. It then produces a list of requested works and their locations. Once you find an interesting gallery you get a map of its whereabouts and opening times.

## Art Guide      www.artguide.org

There are hundreds of magnificent public art collections in the UK and Ireland that are enjoyed by millions of visitors each year. This database contains more than 1,900 named artists, 650 museums and extensive exhibition details.

## Art Historians' Guide to      www.rci.rutgers.edu/
## the Movies      ~eliason/ahgttm.htm

Pop culture meets high art in this unusual catalogue of references to famous works of art and architecture in cinema. Roger Moore sneaking around Egyptian hypostyle halls in *The Spy Who Loved Me*; Ridley Scott's use of Frank Lloyd Wright's Mayan-influenced Ennis Brown house in *Blade Runner* – it's all here. José Ferrer in *Moulin Rouge*, anyone?

## Artcyclopedia      www.artcyclopedia.com

Probably the most comprehensive guide to fine art on the Internet, this is an index of links to 80,000 works by 7,000 different artists, represented at hundreds of museum sites and image archives around the world.

## ArtLex      www.artlex.com

Visual arts dictionary aimed at students, artists and teachers but useful for anyone interested in art. It's organised by technique, period and other terms, so if you're looking for Leonardo, or his Mona Lisa, you're likely to find them under High Renaissance, portrait or sfumato.

### ArtMuseum.net                    www.artmuseum.net
Award-winning Internet-based gallery with major exhibitions, works, and other art-related content online. Surprise surprise, you explore the virtual collections by clicking from one exhibit to another.

### Artnet.com                        www.artnet.com
One of the best places to buy a work of contemporary art. Simply go to the artist index and click on a name to access available works of art from the site's member galleries and artist portfolios.

### Artrepublic.com                   www.artrepublic.com
Art lovers on the move! Enter your travel destination in the search section and you'll get a guide to leading museums and galleries nearby. A concise guide to the history of art spotlights topics from gothic to graffiti.

### Arts Journal                      www.artsjournal.com
Excellent digest covering the best arts and cultural journalism in the English-speaking world. Every day Arts Journal combs through more than 180 English-language publications covering arts and culture, and compiles links to the best.

### Arts & Letters Daily              www.cybereditions.com/aldaily
Very classy effort, collating arts and book reviews from all over the web into a single place where aesthetes will love to hang out.

### Gallery Guide                     www.gallery-guide.com
The most comprehensive source of gallery and museum exhibitions in the United States, organised by geographic areas. There is a useful art world calendar and an Internet Art Directory that provides extensive gallery and museum exhibition details.

### The Great Buildings Collection    www.greatbuildings.com
A gateway to architecture around the world, with a thousand buildings and hundreds of leading architects, 3D models, photographic images and architectural drawings, commentaries, bibliographies, and links for more details of famous structures of all kinds.

**The Grove Dictionary of Art**  www.groveart.com

The printed version is on sale for £5,750, but you can look at it for free here. And goodness, it's a big one, with a staggering 45,000 authoritative articles on every aspect of the visual arts – painting, sculpture, graphic arts, architecture, decorative arts and photography – from prehistory to the present day.

**Islamic Arts and Architecture**  www.islamicart.com

Detailed explanations of the historical and cultural significance of hundreds of Islamic artefacts, with photographs of dozens of works of art, from massive shrines and buildings to tiny silver coins.

**LondonArt**  www.londonart.co.uk

Provides a good introduction to the contemporary art revolution sweeping the capital. Online gallery and auction rooms offer emerging and established artists a platform for the exhibition and sale of their work, while the comprehensive listings service keeps you up-to-date with art shows and events around the world.

**MuseumNet**  www.museums.co.uk

A helpful guide to UK museums, many of which have been reviewed. Search by museum name, region or subject matter.

**Museums around the world**  www.icom.org/vlmp/world.html

This text-heavy but usable page includes an eclectic collection of Internet services connected with museums around the world. The museums are categorised by country or continent. Information and exhibits are in English unless otherwise stated.

**New Exhibitions of**  www.newexhibitions.
**Contemporary Art**  com

Listing of contemporary art exhibitions that can be searched by gallery, artist, exhibition title, by region and, in London and some other cities, by nearest Underground or mainline station. Up-to-date, comprehensive, and free.

**24 Hour Museum**  www.24hourmuseum.org.uk

The UK's best gateway to museums and galleries is well designed and easy-to-use. The Museum Finder makes it easy to locate a gallery in your area. The site lists children's museums and discovery centres, and its Curriculum Navigator has details of stimulating online educational resources.

**WebMuseum**                              **www.southern.net/wm**
You wouldn't know it from the decidedly amateur-looking homepage, but this is actually one of the most useful art history sites on the Internet. And that despite the fact that it doesn't appear to have been updated much since 1996.

---
**Newsgroups**
---

**alt.architecture** – everything from Gaudi to the Guggenheim Bilbao

**alt.art.colleges** – students mix media

**alt.arts.marketplace** – research your next Van Gogh purchase

**alt.binaries.pictures.arts** – excellent source of pix

**rec.arts.fine** – watercolour or oils, discuss your technique here

## //BIOGRAPHIES

*Other people's lives are endlessly fascinating, and a good biography will give insights not just into an individual's life, but also into the times in which they lived.*

**Biography.com**                          **www.biography.com**
The web's foremost biography site lets users explore the lives of the world's most notable personalities, past and present. Features a searchable database of over 20,000 famous names, and message boards where users can share their thoughts on Alexander the Great, Madonna, or whoever they like.

**Britannica's Lives**                     **www.lj.eb.com/lives**
Find out who shared your birthday with this reliable database of biographies of famous people born on a particular date. It's a very

easy page to use – pick a month and day and the site provides matches sorted by birth year, last name or topic – and the results are well written and to the point.

**Distinguished Women of**                 **www.**
**Past and Present**             **distinguishedwomen.com**
Biographies of women who have made significant contributions to the development of society. Search writers, educators, scientists, heads of state, politicians, civil rights crusaders, artists and entertainers by name or subject. Can be a bit earnest at times.

**Forbes Billionaires**            **www.forbes.com/**
**Dictionary**                **tool/toolbox/billnew**
The Internet craze and overheating US stock market turned millionaires into dot.com billionaires in months. Seven of the top ten richest people on Earth are now Americans. Search the world's richest by name, country, or net worth. Each entry includes a short biographical sketch.

**Lives, the Biography Resource**      **http://amillionlives.com**
Biography portal with links to thousands of online biographies, autobiographies, memoirs, diaries and letters. You can search by name or examine biographies about people who share a common profession, historical era or geography.

## //BOOKS

*Whether you want reviews of the latest releases, or are searching for an out-of-print fly fishing classic, the Internet brings the details to your desktop. When the web first exploded as a public medium there was much speculation that it heralded the end of the printed word. But if anything it has ushered in a revival in reading, making it easier to a track down hard-to-find titles.*

**Amazon**                  **www.amazon.co.uk**
Although Amazon is primarily an e-retailer, its excellent reviews, by both readers and site editors, make it a great place to research new

releases and author back catalogues. Its interface is among the most familiar on the Internet, so finding what you are looking for should be easy.

### Bibliofind www.bibliofind.com

Sixteen million used, hard-to-find and rare books offered for sale by thousands of booksellers around the world. Searching is free, and when you find a book you want, use the online order page to purchase it from the bookseller.

### Bibliomania www.bibliomania.com

This superb educational destination has hundreds of searchable full text works of classic fiction, popular fiction, short stories, drama, poetry, dictionaries, research and religious texts, including *Brewer's Phrase and Fable*, *Webster's Dictionary*, *Roget's Thesaurus*, *A Dictionary of Quotations* and (last but not least) the Koran.

### Biblion www.biblion.com

A community of antiquarian and rare booksellers with two main focuses: a store in Mayfair, London where 100 dealers display and sell their stock, and this website where 1000 dealers display and sell theirs. The site makes it easy for collectors to find out about the best of British books.

### The Bookseller www.thebookseller.com

There's a catch. You have to pay £99 for full access to the latest British book news, features, recruitment opportunities, careers information and archives. However, parts are free.

### This British Authors Guide http://incompetech.com/authors

A light and undemanding overview of the major players in British literature. If you already know a lot about the subject you probably won't learn much here, but it'll certainly keep you amused.

### The Internet Book www. Information Centre internetbookinfo.com

This was the first book-related megasite to appear on the Internet, which is why *Publishers Weekly* calls it 'the granddaddy of book-related sites.'

**The New York Times Book Review**  www.nytimes.com/books
Contains daily reviews from the NYT, and a free archive of over 50,000 book reviews dating back to 1980. In addition, you'll find expanded best-seller lists and specials available only on the site, such as audio interviews and features devoted to your favourite authors. Registration is required, but it's free.

**The On-Line Books Page**  http://digital.library.upenn.edu/books
An extensive, if poorly presented, directory of books that can be read for free on the Internet. It includes an index of thousands of online books, pointers to significant directories and archives of other online texts.

**Project Gutenberg**  http://promo.net/pg
This site makes information, books and other materials available to the general public in forms the vast majority people can easily read, use, quote and search. There are three portions to the site's vast library: light literature, heavy literature and a set of encyclopedia and dictionaries.

---

### Newsgroups

---

**alt.books** – review, recommend and discuss

**alt.book.reviews** – 'If you want to know how it turns out, read it!'

**rec.arts.books** – books of all genres, and the publishing industry

**rec.arts.books.tolkien** – Frodo, Bilbo, Gandalf and friends

**rec.collecting.books** – issues related to collecting books of all types

## //CALCULATION & CONVERSION

*One and one equals two, but if you need your trusty old calculator to do anything more sophisticated you may be in trouble.*

*Thankfully the Internet is full of useful sites to help you calculate everything from your salary to your body temperature and holiday money requirements. Your old pocket calculator has never seemed so ancient.*

**Calculator.com**                    **www.calculator.com**
Free access to online calculators to help you solve problems and answer questions. There are specialist calculators for finance, business, and science, cooking, hobbies, and health. Some solve problems, others satisfy curiosity, but all attempt to put the answer easily within reach.

**Dictionary of Units     www.ex.ac.uk/cimt/dictunit/dictunit.htm**
How long is a piece of string? This site provides a summary of most of the units of measurement to be found in use around the world today (and a few of historical interest), together with the appropriate conversion factors needed to change them into a standard SI unit like metres or centimetres.

**The FootRule**                    **www.omnis.demon.co.uk**
A continuously expanding collection of converters, units and measures, data tables and facilities. The converters tell you things like how many miles make a light year; the site also gives the invaluable background on units, their origin and definitions.

**The Love Calculator**                    **www.lovecalculator.com**
The Love Doctor himself must have designed this completely useless machine. The site lets you calculate the probability of a successful relationship between two people and makes the highly suspect claim that it can tell whether your relationships will last or not.

**Payslip**                    **www.digita.com/**
**Calculator**                    **content/tools/calculators/payslip**
UK readers can use this site to check tax and National Insurance contributions deducted from pay in a normal week or month. It's one of a large number of useful tools on this site.

**Roman Numeral Converter**  www.binary.net/dturley/js/roman.html

This site converts Roman to Arabic numbers. The Roman number input must be all in capital letters. While you're there, it's worth checking out the site's Shakespearean insult generator.

**Temperature converter**  www.cchem.berkeley.edu/ChemResources/temperature.html

This site lets you convert Fahrenheit, Kelvin and Réaumur temperatures into Centigrade and vice versa.

**The Travel-Finder Calculator**  www.travel-finder.com/convert

Select the amount to convert, the original currency units and the desired currency units, then click convert. Usefully, the calculator stays in a pop-up window until you close it.

**The Universal Currency Converter**  www.xe.net/ucc

Allows you to convert foreign exchange rates on the Internet. Select the source and destination currencies using the scrolling selection boxes, push the 'Perform Currency Conversion' button, and your results are displayed. Note that there are far more currencies available than those initially displayed.

## //CARS

*If you're thinking about buying a new or used car the net lets you look up information for just about every make or model. You'll find all the facts and figures online, with none of the brochures or overly persistent sales patter. Compare features, equipment and see the advantages of one car over another. Try simply placing the make in your browser's address window, add a co.uk or .com and see where that takes you. As a rule .com URLs will take you to the company's US site. If you still can't find the make you're looking for use one of the major search engines.*

**Autobytel**  www.autobytel.co.uk

As much information as you need in order to make your car-buying decision easier. This is a great destination for anyone researching a new car. Look at up to three cars side by side, or use the site to get some help choosing.

### Autohit                                    www.autohit.com
Use this popular UK site to sell your current vehicle and research, identify, finance, insure and buy your next. You can have your car valued, get the latest new model news and find a dealer in your area. The site has a review of current motoring reports and an excellent series of links to manufacturers, owner groups, clubs and other motoring related Internet resources.

### The AUTOmotive encycloPEDIA              http://autopedia.com
All manner of information related to cars, boats, trucks, motorcycles and off-roaders. Material is geared to American users, although general tips on financing, negotiating and buying a used car are pretty universal.

### Carbusters                                www.carbusters.com
If you want to save money on UK dealer list prices, this site can help you find a new car in Europe and import it back into the UK.

### Cars.com                                    www.cars.com
A search engine for cars. You can look for information on new and used models, read up on car tests and compare various models of car – this comparison feature allows you to perform a side-by-side comparison of up to four new US vehicles. There's also useful material on car ownership.

### CarsDirect                                www.carsdirect.com
Research and compare cars and work how much car you can afford. You can search by manufacturer, price, vehicle type, or all of these. If you find a car you like you can buy it thorough the site – providing you live in the US.

### Carseekers                              www.carseekers.co.uk
A group of private motorists fed up with high UK car prices set up this service. Thanks to this site you can reap the benefit of buying

where prices are lower, whilst they act as agents to help with the purchase, delivery and legal processes.

**Drive**　　　　　　　　　　　　　**www.drive.com.au**
Everything the Aussie motorist will ever need to know. The news section has a car library with hundreds of articles and consumer reports. You can get accurate valuations of used cars while checking out the credentials of the dealer, and compare new cars specs and prices.

**Exchange and Mart**　　　　**www.exchangeandmart.co.uk**
Brings one of the UK's major sources of used cars to the net. Choose the make, model, and region you're interested in and hey presto! At least, that's the theory.

**Which? Motoring**　　　　　　**www.which.net/motoring**
Tests for the things that really matter like reliability, as well as campaigning to bring down car prices and increase car safety. Divided into two main areas – a free site available to anyone, and a subscriber area you can only access if you have a password.

---

**Newsgroups**

---

**aus.car** – automobiles in Australia

**rec.autos.antique** – cars over 25 years old

**uk.rec.cars.maintenance** – general car maintenance

**uk.rec.cars.modification** – what you can and can't do

## //COMPUTERS & THE INTERNET

*It's only natural to turn to the Internet for computer advice. The geeks who built it have posted a huge variety of tips and tricks to make using your computer a hassle-free affair. One thing everyone who becomes an Internet obsessive remarks on is the phenomenal pace of change within the industry. To keep on top of the latest buzz words, you'll want to visit the technological news sites here regularly. And on the Internet that means hourly rather than once or twice a week.*

### About-the-web     http://about-the-web.com
A good starting point, offering lots of information on browsers, email programs, newsgroups, search engines, avoiding scams, web page creation, money making opportunities, creating and promoting websites and tips for a better web surfing experience.

### Apple     www.apple.com
Research all the latest hardware from the makers of the iMac. A beautifully designed site, this does a great job selling and promoting Apple's laptop and desktop computers. The care service and support should be able to answer all your questions.

### Builder.com     www.builder.com
This huge, regularly updated destination has news, reviews and advice on every single aspect of website building. It's probably not the place to come if you're a complete beginner, but if you know your Dreamweaver from your Adobe Illustrator you'll find everything you need to make your site the next Amazon.com.

### Cnet     www.cnet.com
Hugely comprehensive site with just about everything you could ever wish to know about computers. Software reviews, analysis on the latest cutting-edge technology trends, help and how-to guides, this site has it all. You can also request weekly emails from the team, updating you on all the latest developments.

### The Computer History Centre     www.computerhistory.org
This site provides an easily accessible centre for anyone needing to research the history of computing. A useful timeline explores this history from 1945 to 1990.

### Creating Killer Websites     www.killersites.com
Based on a best-selling book, this complementary site is packed with updated information on designing for the latest browsers,

solutions from the top web design firms around the world and new HTML tips and tricks.

**Download** www.download.com

The single best place on the net for downloads and a fantastic place to get clear, unbiased advice on whether or even why you might need a particular piece of software. Popular downloads include packages designed to speed up your web connection.

**Encyclopedia of the** http://hotwired.lycos.
**New Economy** com/special/ene

Created by *Wired* magazine, this exhaustive and topical encyclopedia discusses topics ranging from 'adhocracy' to distributed systems, ECash to Netscape, and network externalities to zero sum. The essays are wonderfully tongue-in-cheek, but they still manage to present useful descriptions and definitions.

**Experts Exchange** www.expertsexchange.com

With over 300,000 members this site has a huge community of computer experts ready to answer your specific questions. There's a useful collection of PAQ's (previously asked questions) and 1.5 million searchable postings, one of which may instantly answer your question.

**HotWired** www.hotwired.com

Award-winning site covering web technology and culture, catering mainly for the web's large, emerging class of 'participants' – professionals and enthusiasts who are actively involved in creating the web and have made the medium a part of their lives.

**The Industry Standard** www.thestandard.com

Written for senior-level executives who view the Internet as an opportunity to grow their business, this site delivers sophisticated coverage of the people, companies and business models shaping the new economy.

**Internet for Beginners** http://netforbeginners.about.com

Covering everything from browsers to the Usenet, via high speed access and a concise guide to Internet jargon, this site is approachable and non-intimidating, and filled with useful information for beginners. One of the best destinations to learn the basics.

**InternetStats.com**  www.internetstats.com
A very well presented site that helps point marketers, entrepreneurs and professionals to sites that have the information, statistics, trends and news they are looking for. Use it as a guide to save time when conducting research online.

**The Internet Traffic Report**  www.internettrafficreport.com
Monitors the flow of data around the world to show where has the fastest and most reliable connections. You can view graphs or click on a continent for more detailed information.

**Introduction to**  www.utoronto.ca/
**HTML**  webdocs/HTMLdocs/NewHTML/htmlindex.html
Useful collection of documents designed for developers interested in learning HTML. Contains an overview and description of the HTML language (including a discussion of URLs). There are extensive references and useful guides to other online resources.

**Microsoft**  www.microsoft.com
This site, as well as being a showcase for Bill's vast product range, is also the best place to come for news of future releases and operating system upgrades. There is a well-used technical help section.

**The NCSA Beginner's**  www.ncsa.uiuc.edu/General/Internet/
**Guide to HTML**  WWW/HTMLPrimer.html
Use this as a starting point to understanding the language of the World Wide Web. As an introduction, the site does not pretend to offer instructions on every aspect of HTML, but it has plenty of useful hints.

**NetGuide**  www.netguide.com/HowTo
A straightforward guide to doing more on the Internet. New sites, best sites, live events, Internet tips and tricks – this site provide

everything you need to know to get the most out of your online experience.

**NetLingo** www.netlingo.com

If you're puzzled by anything you read on or about the web, come here. NetLingo bills itself as the 'Internet language dictionary', and it's a leading lexicon for people who want practical information about technology, computing and the online world.

**Network Solutions** www.networksolutions.com

All about finding and registering domain names. Use partner site www.dotcomdirectory.com to find businesses online by type, name or web address.

**PC Direct** www.pcdirect.co.uk

Online version of one of the UK's most popular computer magazine. If you're thinking of buying some computer gear this is a good place to compare products. And unlike the magazine, it's free.

**Red Herring** www.redherring.com

Well-informed analysis and commentary on the business of technology from industry insiders. This site explains how technology business news and events affect you, your industry, the economy, the stock market, and your portfolio.

**The Register** www.theregister.co.uk

Unmissable. 'Biting the hand that feeds IT,' this is a satirical, wickedly funny look at the day's technology news. Despite – or more probably, because of – its tongue in cheek approach, this is the single best source of tech news in the UK.

**Search Engine Watch** www.searchenginewatch.com

How search engines work and how they can help you find things. The site compiles all the latest news and search engine statistics to keep you fully up to speed with developments in these vital research tools.

**Slashdot**                                    www.slashdot.org

Offering 'news for nerds' on 'stuff that matters', this series of rolling bulletin boards is a good place to keep up to date with the rapid pace of today's technological changes. The site is easy to get around, very accessible and covers a huge range of topics.

**The Tech Encyclopedia**          www.techweb.com/encyclopedia

This useful site has more than 14,000 definitions of computer terms and concepts. The source for this encyclopedia is The Computer Desktop Encyclopedia. You can download a free demo of the multimedia version here.

**The Web Design Group**                        www.htmlhelp.com

A practical site that offers useful advice on web design topics. Use this site to make sure you create sites that can be used by every Internet user, regardless of their computer or browser.

**Web Developers Virtual Library**                  www.wdvl.com

If you are new to the net and are looking to build your first website, this is a great resource. There's everything you need to get started, from explanations of the Internet, the World Wide Web and HTML to a catalogue of web-based tutorials.

**WebDeveloper.com**                        www.webdeveloper.com

You ask the tough web development questions. This site supplies answers. There's an excellent Java script tutorial, advice on running banner ads on your site and how-to instructions for everything from basic HTML to cascading style sheets.

**Webmonkey**              http://hotwired.lycos.com/webmonkey

Highly acclaimed site from the *Wired* magazine stable that teaches you how to put the latest web developments to use on a daily basis.

**Webopedia**                      http://webopedia.internet.com

This reference site is perhaps more justified than NetLingo in its claim to be the only online dictionary you need for computer and Internet technology. The excellent quick reference section has concise and practical information.

**Webpages That Suck**  www.webpagesthatsuck.com
How not to do it. The idea is to teach you good design by looking at bad design, and some of the examples are truly terrible. Also gives excellent tips on making your site successful.

**WebWise**  www.bbc.co.uk/webwise
BBC Education's excellent online introductory guide to the Internet, with over 1,000 pages of help, tips and plain-speaking advice. This is a good place to start if you're new to the net, or want to expand your knowledge and skill base once the basics are in place. Click on Bruce, the WebWise spider, if you're lost and want to get back to the homepage.

**Whatis.com**  www.whatis.com
A comprehensive information technology guide with 2,000 individual encyclopedic definitions and a number of quick-reference pages. Topics are cross-referenced between definitions and to other sites for further information. The interactive tour provides a good general introduction to the infrastructure of the net.

**Wired News**  www.wired.com/news
A great source of daily news and analysis of the technologies, companies, and people driving the information age. *Wired* magazine has won a reputation for delivering an insider's perspective on how technology affects society, making this a great place to keep up to speed.

**ZDNet UK**  www.zdnet.co.uk
Combining the best of the Ziff-Davis computer magazine titles, this is probably the best place to begin researching any computer-related matter. There are excellent guides to unmetered net access, and detailed computer reviews and product information.

---

**Newsgroups**

---

**alt.comp.shareware** – share that software

**alt.comp.virus** – keep yourself clean

**alt.html** – for web page building junkies

**alt.security** – build yourself a firewall

**alt.windows98** – for its friends and enemies

**comp.infosystems.www.misc** – general web-related chat

**comp.lang.java** – talk to other Java freaks

**comp.newprod** – get the insiders' perspective on the latest hard and software

**comp.sys.mac.hardware** – how to keep your iMac ticking over

**comp.virus** – make sure you don't catch the love bug

## //CONSUMER INFORMATION

*Whether you feel you're being ripped off by your telephone company or are unsure about what the label on your child's baby food actually means, the Internet should be able to answer your queries. With so many things to buy, and so many ways of paying, you can be forgiven for feeling a little bit confused now and again. Let these excellent consumer information sites ease your worries.*

**The Consumer Gateway**  www.consumer.gov.uk
British government portal that links to sites containing consumer information and advice. Because they've been vetted by the government, you can be sure that the sites provide quality advice and information, as well as access to practical assistance.

**Consumer Reports**  www.consumerreports.org
Huge site that publishes the findings of the US Consumers Union, an independent non-profit organisation that tests products in order to protect consumers. This is a comprehensive source of unbiased advice about personal finance, health and nutrition – in fact products and services of all kinds.

**Consumer World**                    www.consumerworld.org
A public service, non-commercial guide that catalogues over 2000 or the Internet's most useful consumer related sites. Lots of advice and a weekly newsletter on consumer news stories, features, and bargains.

**Consumers Association of Canada**          www.consumer.ca
A rather functional site, but the CA publishes an endless series of reports into topics such as food labelling, health care services, electrical safety standards, fuel prices, pensions, insurance and the performance of the utility sector.

**National Consumer Website**          www.consumer.gov.au
Consumer affairs and fair-trading matters for both Australia and New Zealand. There's an excellent guide to 'keeping baby safe' and the Little Book of Scams, which provides a consumers guide to 'scams, swindles, rorts and rip offs.'

**The Office of Fair Trading**              www.oft.gov.uk
This noble organisation sets out to protect British consumers, and make sure there is full and open competition between companies. You'll find advice on shopping on the Internet, tips on buying a used car and guides to a wide range of topics, including student and personal finance.

**Trading Standards Net**          www.tradingstandards.net
Contains a wide range of current and reference information for consumers with a query or complaint, or businesses that want to know about their legal obligations in this field.

**US Consumer Gateway**                    www.consumer.gov
This site links to a broad range of federal information resources available online. It's designed so that you can locate information by category – these include food, health, product safety, and transportation. ScamAlert provides details of fraudulent practices in the marketplace.

**Which?**                                          **www.which.net**

This site provides everything you'd expect from the Consumers Association, which was set up to improve the standard of goods and services in the UK. The online reports are published at the same time as the printed versions. The site has interactive features that allow users to contribute to research consumer issues and share their findings with other site visitors.

---

**Newsgroups**

---

**alt.consumers.experiences** – report what rubs you up

**aus.consumers** – Oz consumer stuff

**can.consumers** – Canadian consumer interests

**misc.consumers** – product reviews and more

**uk.people.consumers** – UK-based discussion of products and services

## //DATE & TIME

*In some ways, time has no meaning on the Internet. You can wake up in New York and turn on the late night radio in Tokyo. Some talking heads have imagined a not-too-distant future where accountants in Shanghai balance the books overnight for companies in London. All the same, there's plenty of information on the web about time and times: find out the significance of the leap second, and (on a more practical note) make sure you know about public holidays before you set off on business or pleasure.*

**Britannica Clockworks**          **www.britannica.com/clockworks**

Stimulating site that charts the development of timekeeping from the sundial to the atomic clock, clearly explaining the instruments that measure the days and demonstrating the importance of time in the development of science and civilisation.

**Calendar Zone**                     www.calendarzone.com

This vast site has links to more calendrical issues than you would ever have imagined existed. Typical fare includes a discussion of the impact and influence of the Mayan calendar, seasonal festivities of the Greeks and Romans and a look at the Pagan calendar.

**Daily Globe**                          www.dailyglobe.com

Immense collection of links that includes specific calendar systems divided into days, weeks, months and years, comparisons of the major calendars, lunar, solar and ecclesiastical calendars plus a revealing look at the Moon's influence on calendars.

**Date and Time Gateway**                   www.bsdi.com/date

Just what you always wanted: the exact Greenwich Mean Time for the instant you accessed the page. There is also local time information for hundreds of cities, which are (rather confusingly) grouped into both countries and geographic areas.

**Interfaith Calendar**              www.interfaithcalendar.org

All the dates for sacred celebrations and spiritual holidays around the world for the next five years. You can search by religion or year, and the site also has a helpful alphabetical list of sacred calendar terms, with brief descriptions.

**Leap Seconds**          http://tycho.usno.navy.mil/leapsec.html

To ensure that the uniform time scale defined by the world's atomic clocks stays in step with the Earth's slightly erratic revolutions, the time is occasionally adjusted by single-second increments. This site carries a detailed explanation of what a second actually is, explaining why leap seconds are necessary.

**Time and Date**                       www.timeanddate.com

If it is 9 am in Sydney, what time is it elsewhere? This service helps you find out. Past or present, it can show corresponding local times around the world for the time selected. Useful if you have contacts all over the world, and often have to check local time.

**Time Zone Converter**       www.timezoneconverter.com

As you'd expect from the name, this is a good place to find out the time anywhere in the world.

**The Worldwide Holiday and**       www.holidayfestival.
**Festival Site**       com

Have you ever travelled abroad only to find on arrival that the places you wanted to visit are all shut, or that public holidays have cut your five days work down to two? This site brings together information on holidays around the world.

## //DICTIONARIES & THESAURI

*The Internet can replace a whole shelf of standard reference books. These sites are often quicker to use than their paper equivalents, and the links make it especially easy to jump from one word to another.*

**AllWords.com**       www.allwords.com

Designed to look like a bookshelf, this helpful site is an English dictionary with multi-lingual search. So definitions and pronunciations are only in English, but you can search for and display the resulting words in German, French, Spanish, Dutch and Italian.

**The Alternative**       www.notam.uio.no/~
**Dictionaries**       hcholm/altlang

Parental Advisory: this is one of the few reference and research sites with an '18 certificate,' containing words and expressions you wouldn't find in a normal dictionary including slang, insults, racial slurs, and terms for bodily functions.

**Cambridge Dictionaries**    http://uk.cambridge.org/esl/dictionary

Use this simple page to start your search of the combined texts of the International Dictionary of Idioms, the International Dictionary of English and International Dictionary of Phrasal Verbs.

**Dictionaries and**      **www.niss.ac.uk/**
**reference works**      **lis/dictres.html**
Useful selection of links to online general reference works –
including maps and encyclopedias as well as dictionaries. The
service comes from the UK's National Information Services and
Systems (NISS for short).

**Dictionary.com**      **www.dictionary.com**
One of the most popular and easy to use dictionary services on the
net. Each search scans through a selection of online dictionaries. If
you have a question about words, grammar or language you can
use the Ask Dr Dictionary feature.

**Dictionary of Cell and**      **http://on.to/**
**Molecular Biology**      **dictionary**
Quick access to clearly explained, cross-referenced definitions of
terms encountered in modern biology. It contains 7,072 entries and
7,168 cross-references, ranging from genes and DNA to membrane
trafficking.

**The Dictionary of**      **www.bibliomania.com/**
**Phrase and Fable**      **Reference/PhraseAndFable**
Dr Brewer's classic work of reference has been in popular demand
since 1870, but the good doctor could never have imagined that his
cross-references would be turned into hyperlinks and his dictionary
be accessible by computer.

**The Early Modern English**      **www.chass.utoronto.ca/**
**Dictionaries Database**      **english/emed/emedd.html**
For anyone researching the origins of Modern English – particularly students of Shakespeare – this is an accessible collection of
eleven bilingual and monolingual dictionaries published between
1530 to 1657.

**English as a second language**      **http://pages.**
**for Americans**      **prodigy.com/NY/NYC/britspk**
It isn't easy being British. Having to keep a stiff upper lip all the

time. Struggling to get that accent right. The folks at the BritSpeak language laboratory invite you to grab your brolly and join them on an illuminating linguistic tour of Britain, but they haven't updated the site since 1997.

**OneLook Dictionaries**                    www.onelook.com
One Look searches a broad range of dictionaries simultaneously, making it much easier to find the right answer. There's also an excellent list of links to a huge range of specialised online dictionaries.

**The Online Medical Dictionary**      www.graylab.ac.uk/omd
Acronyms, jargon, theory, standards and history – in fact anything to do with medicine or science. Search by the first letter of a term, or by subject areas covering everything from anatomy to zoology.

**Oxford English Dictionary**                  www.oed.com
The undisputed authority on the history and development of the English language, with unbeatable information on the evolution of words and meanings from the earliest times to the present day. Now available online for £350 a year – worth it if you're really into words.

**The Phrase Finder**      www.shu.ac.uk/web-admin/phrases
Don't let finding phrases become a 'labour of love,' instead employ this searchable database of English phrases, sayings and clichés, which takes every word you give it and produces a list of (at times, only vaguely) related phrases.

**Symbols.com**                              www.symbols.com
A stunning, highly informative site for the world's largest online encyclopedia of graphic symbols, with more than 2,500 signs arranged into groups of different shapes and styles. Symbols covered range from ideograms carved in mammoth teeth by Cro-Magnon men, to hobo signs, swastikas and subway graffiti.

**Thesaurus.com**                          www.thesaurus.com
Browse, skim, riffle, dip or leaf through different ways of saying the

same thing, either through the alphabetical index of keywords or through the six broad categories into which the original thesaurist, Mr Roget himself, classified the entire English vocabulary.

## //ENCYCLOPEDIAS

*Whether you're looking for specific information about something obscure, or a concise explanation of something simple, the Internet's countless encyclopedias can help. You can learn all you want about gnomes, leprechauns and fairies; find sites dedicated to the history of the violin, Kung Fu or medicinal herbs; and discover others that answer every DIY question imaginable.*

**Britannica**                                     **www.britannica.com**
For more than 200 years Encyclopedia Britannica has been the world leader in reference publishing. Of all the electronic encyclopedias available today, none can match this for breadth of knowledge, quality of information and sheer research power. Once you've entered your query, the site returns a selection of encyclopedia entries, learned articles held in their database and related sites recommended by Britannica's very clever editors.

**Bushido Martial Arts Encyclopedia**              **www.bushido.ch**
Specialist, but good. Bushido, literally the 'Way of the Warrior', was the code of the samurai, and is the starting point for all martial arts. This excellent encyclopedia explores its history and philosophy, including its relation to Kung Fu and Karate.

**Catholic Encyclopedia**            **www.newadvent.org/cathen**
This site was created in reaction to a spate of new encyclopedias that either ignored Catholic issues or got them wrong. If you can find any gaps here, the editors have to say 500 Hail Maries. Just kidding.

**Columbia Encyclopedia**                **www.bartleby.com/65/**
With over 50,000 article entries, 40,000 bibliographic citations, and 80,000 cross-referenced entries, this 6th edition contains more data

than many multi-volume encyclopedias. The *New York Times Book Review* called it 'the standard of excellence as a guide to essential facts,' and it's hard to disagree.

**Compton's Encyclopedia Online**          www.comptons.com
Detailed and richly cross-referenced information on almost any topic you want to explore, and more than 16,000 pictures, flags, maps, and charts, as well as tables and MIDI and other sound files.

**Encarta**          http://encarta.msn.com
Showcases the depth of Microsoft's award-winning reference products, with 16,000 free articles, multimedia and access to the Encarta dictionary. The site works like a search engine, with three search fields and a choice of some specific categories.

**Encyclopedia.com**          www.encyclopedia.com
Based on The Concise Columbia Encyclopedia, this site provides current information available in all major fields of knowledge – from politics, law, art, and history to sports, literature, geography, science, and medicine. There's also the option of expanding your research to other related sites.

**The Encyclopedia Mythica**          www.pantheon.org/mythica
A massive site with 5,700 definitions of gods, supernatural beings, legendary creatures and monsters from around the world. Topics covered include animals such as unicorns and dragons; objects like Excalibur, imaginative places such as Atlantis and Avalon, and supernatural creatures such as gnomes, leprechauns, and fairies.

**Encyclopedia of Animals**    www.funkandwagnalls.com/animals
Loads of animal images, and concise but detailed descriptions of every kind of beast and their habitats.

**The Encyclopedia of the Orient**          http://i-cias.com/e.o
Not quite what the name would lead you to believe, as it stops well short of Japan. It does, however, cover all countries and cultures between Morocco and Iran. This excellent site does a good job presenting all aspects of one of the world's most interesting regions.

**Encyclopedia Smithsonian**   www.si.edu/resource/faq/start.htm

Washington's Smithsonian Institution receives many public inquiries covering a wide range of topics, and this site sets out to answer them. The huge variety of topics include military history, anthropology, mineral sciences, musical history, physical sciences, services, textiles conservation, transportation history, and vertebrate zoology.

**EncycloZine**   http://encyclozine.com

Stunningly illustrated encyclopedic portal that covers a wide range of topics in the arts, humanities, sciences and technology. It features quizzes and galleries of art, fractals, space, optical illusions. Worth a visit for the photographs alone.

**Funk & Wagnalls**   www.funkandwagnalls.com

The focus of this site is the comprehensive coverage of current events. There is also complete access to Funk & Wagnalls unabridged 29-volume encyclopedia, with lots of animation, sounds, music, flags and maps to bring everything to life.

**The Herbal Encyclopedia**   www.wic.net/waltzark/herbenc.htm

Answers many questions about herbs in cookery and medicine. Organised into sections covering aromatherapy, recipes, rituals and how to gather and store herbs.

**The Home Improvement Encyclopedia**   www.bhg.com/homeimp

DIY experts show you how to accomplish almost anything related to improving your home – after pointing out that they are not liable if anything goes wrong. The Encyclopedia is divided into four main topics: plumbing, wiring, carpentry, decks and masonry and concrete.

**How Stuff Works**   www.howstuffworks.com

The average Western citizen has access to technology inconceivable a century ago, but do we understand how these wonders of modern life work? If you've ever pondered how the news appears on your TV, or marvelled at modern telephony, this site shows you how it's done.

**Instrument Encyclopedia**
www.si.umich.edu/CHICO/MHN/enclpdia.html

Good guide to musical instruments from around the world. Browse by geographical origin to learn more about your favourite instrument, or use the Sachs-Hornbostel classification scheme. To find out what that is, you'll have to go there. There's also a glossary of musical terms and information about museum instrument collections.

**Women's History Encyclopedia**
www.teleport.com/~megaines/women.html

This project began as a classroom assignment to write research papers on prominent female figures, and has grown into a collective celebration of women's history. An intriguing and useful starting point for further research.

## //ENTERTAINMENT

*Find out about the latest movie releases, about what is going on in your area or see gigs and shows online as they happen. Don't expect to find out what's on TV easily, but cinema listings are much better. Online entertainment is in its infancy, but with the emergence of new technologies like handheld video phones, our entertainment choices are changing dramatically.*

**Ananova**
www.ananova.com

A mammoth database lists all the major UK entertainment events. Search by town, title or venue for full details of what's on in cinema, theatre, rock and pop, classical music, opera, dance, comedy, clubs and visual art. There's also childrens' events and tourist attractions. For many events, Ananova gives you the chance to snap up tickets online as soon as they become available.

**BBC Alert!**
www.bbc.co.uk/alert

You'll never have to trawl through the *Radio Times* ever again. Alert does all the work for you. Simply tell them what interests you and they will email you your own personalised TV and Radio listings every week.

**Culture Finder**                                      **www.culturefinder.com**

A deserving two-time winner of Yahoo! Internet Life magazine's best cultural events category, this enormous yet easy-to-use site is the leading arts ticketing and cultural information site for the US and Canada. It provides an unparalleled array of listings, with access to online tickets for arts events across every genres imaginable. Site visitors can look for opera events in Chicago; Broadway hits in New York; orchestra performances in San Francisco, or thousands of other events in over 1,500 North American cities. Why go anywhere else?

**EntsWeb**                                                **www.entsweb.co.uk**

This is a tightly focused specialist resource for anyone booking entertainers for a party, ball, gig ... whatever. Each section breaks down into subsections. So the musicians category covers everything from tribute bands to Elizabethan minstrels.

**The Gateway to**                                        **www.go-edinburgh.**
**Edinburgh's Festivals**                                       **co.uk**

Edinburgh is a year-round city of festivals, ranging from Hogmanay to the world famous fringe. Use this portal to access the individual festival sites, find out how and when their programmes are available, and search events online.

**Gigs and Tours**       **www.broadband.co.uk/wayahead/web/sjm**

Commercial site orientated towards ticket sales, but nevertheless a good way to find out what bands are touring when (and where). It then becomes an added convenience if you decide you want tickets for the show.

**Scour**                                                      **www.scour.net**

Details of every kind of music (including streaming radio stations), movies and videos from all over the world.

**TheatreNet.com**  www.theatrenet.com

Good-looking guide to the UK theatre scene. News archive, links to theatres, reviews for the current hit shows – and a chance to book online – make this one of the best places to work out what to see. Most of the information is on the (very long) homepage.

**What's On Stage**  www.whatsonstage.com

Claims to be the UK's largest database of theatre, opera, classical, dance, ballet and pantomime events. Allows you to check on more than 2,000 performances around the country. The dense, text-heavy front page gives a confusing number of options, but does include searches by place or time.

**Whatsonwhen**  www.whatsonwhen.com

Search the world's best events. This site doesn't aim to cover every event in the world, but if there's something happening that you might want to travel to see (or wouldn't want to miss if you're in the area) they've probably got it covered.

---

**Newsgroups**

---

**alt.tv.ab-fab** – yes, sweetie (and scroll down for just about every show you can think of)

**alt.cable-tv** – what's on, what's coming, what's it like?

**rec.arts.tv.soaps** – all the latest from the Street, the Square and the Close

**rec.arts.tv.uk** – general UK television discussion

**uk.culture.arts.theatre** – who's treading the boards?

## //FOOD & DRINK

*Pineapple bacon burgers. Oyster mushrooms. Fried spinach, spiced ice coffee, triple layer carrot cake, gunkan sushi – whether you're searching for a new recipe to impress your dinner guests, or trying to check if that mushroom you picked is edible, the Internet brings you what you need to know.*

**AllRecipes.com**                    **www.allrecipes.com**

America's leading food community, recipe-finder and meal planning site offers users everything about nosh. A popular feature on the site is 'My Recipe Box', which allows you to store, organise and share your favourite dishes.

**Chopstix**                    **www.chopstix.co.uk**

It's not just chop suey, sesame prawn toast and crispy fried duck – as you will find out here as you brush up on Chinese lifestyle, culture and foodstuffs. If you're looking for a particular dish, you'll probably find the recipe in the excellent searchable database.

**Coffee World**                    **www.realcoffee.co.uk**

Make mine a double decaff vanilla-flavoured Americano. Wake up and smell the website that explores the evolution of this invaluable drink. The site describes the most popular methods of making coffee, showing how to get the best out of your cafetière, drip filter or percolator, and has a glossary that explains aroma and the difference between espresso and latte.

**Epicurious**                    **www.epicurious.com**

Know satay from sauté, semifreddo from spoom? The exhaustive dictionary of more than 4,000 food terms means you'll never have to eat your words. There are metric equivalents and a herb-and-spice chart in the sites reference guides, but the heart of the site is a bank of more than 10,000 recipes from *Gourmet* and *Bon Appetit*, America's most popular food magazines.

**Food Lovers Glossary**                    **www.foodstuff.com**

From *A la minute* to *Zuppa Inglese*, this excellent glossary has got it covered. This is a useful site that will have something for you whether you came to browse the pantry shelves, look up a food term or discover a new recipe.

**IDrink The Drink Mixing Website**　　　www.idrink.com
Tell the site what you've got in your drinks cabinet, and it suggests what you can do with it – mainly cocktails, from traditional favourites to the latest trendy concoctions. There are thousands of drinks recipes here, compiled from recipes submitted by professional and amateur bartenders. That's a lot of different ways to get drunk.

**Inside Sushi**　　　www.learn-sushi.com
The training is hard. For the first two years, you sweep the floor. The second two, you sharpen the knives – and that's before you even get to touch the fish itself. This site, part of the LearnFree.com network, provides plenty of useful information about this sometimes intimidating raw-fish-and-rice speciality.

**The Mushroom Council**　　　www.mushroomcouncil.com
There are over 2,500 mushroom varieties grown in the world today. Use this beautiful site to learn more about exotic types like oyster mushrooms and beech mushrooms. Also has tips on cooking with fungi, simple ideas to dress up a meal with fresh mushrooms, and how-to guides to cleaning, preparing and storing them.

**Scotch Whisky**　　　www.scotchwhisky.com
There are few products so closely related to the land of their birth than Scotch whisky. It is the lifeblood of Scotland, and has become one of the most popular spirits in the world. This site, best viewed with a tumbler of the true water in your hand, looks at the history and processes of making this king of spirits.

**The Soil Association**　　　www.soilassociation.org
Organic farming aims to maintain the long-term fertility of the soil and use fewer of the earth's resources to produce tasty, healthy food. This site explains why you should go organic, has a comprehensive library of previously published reports and gives tips on where to find organic food.

**The Spice Encyclopedia**  www.spiceguide.com

Fascinating facts and useful ideas to inspire your own cooking adventures. From allspice to vanilla, the site makes creative cooking easy and fun, while explaining the dramatic role of herbs and spices in the development of Western civilisation.

**Teatime.com**  www.teatime.com

Parts of this site have not been updated for quite some time, but there is still plenty of good information. As well as listing tea types and vendors, it boasts an excellent tea terms glossary which explains the origins of words like chai and teas such as Earl Grey.

**Tom Cannavan's Wine Pages**  www.wine-pages.com

Run by the IT manager at Glasgow University, this site bears the mark of the serious enthusiast, with technical knowledge engagingly presented. More than 1,000 tasting notes, essays, book reviews, vintage charts and tips on food and wine pairings.

**The Ultimate Directory of Cooking Sites**  www.tudocs.com

Follow the links to an excellent specialist directory of cookery sites on the web, designed to take you to the exact recipe or cooking information you want while giving you an idea of what you might expect. The list is searchable by food type, and sites are rated out of five.

**Wine Spectator**  www.winespectator.com

This is America's biggest wine site, and it's tremendously useful. The ratings database has scores and descriptions for more than 83,000 wines. You can see tasting notes for wines rated during the past two years for free.

---

**Newsgroups**

---

**alt.beer** – get some froth on your moustache

**alt.food** – food in all its glory

**alt.food.fat-free** – food without the trimmings

**alt.food.wine** – what goes well with what, for oenophiles

**rec.crafts.winemaking** – maintain your own vineyard

**rec.food.cooking** – be the next Marco Pierre White

**rec.food.preserving** – preserving foodstuffs and herbs

**rec.food.recipes** – share your favourites

**rec.food.veg.cooking** – food without the recently living trimmings

**uk.food+drink.real-ale** – cask-conditioned ales

## //GARDENING

*The typical gardener, dedicated to the soil to the point of distraction, is often no less obsessive than the computer enthusiast. So it's no surprise to find a huge range of gardening information available online.*

**British Wildflower Plants**          www.wildflowers.co.uk
One of the largest providers of wildflower plants in the UK, this site also has a searchable database (common and scientific names) of plants illustrated with hundreds of beautiful photographs.

**Dig-it.co.uk**          www.dig-it.co.uk
A nice destination for basic gardening information, coupled with the chance to buy, this good-looking site has an extensive plant finder with more than 500 varieties. There is also an informative glossary of terms, and members can ask expert gardeners for advice.

**E-garden**          www.e-garden.co.uk
Slow loading, image-heavy site that still manages to deliver. Content includes seasonal gardening tips and an image library. The three-day weather forecasts help to ensure you don't start digging up your garden minutes before monsoon rains pour down.

**The Encyclopedia of Plants**  www.botany.com

Tons of information about methods of cultivation, soil and temperature requirements and other important matters. The directory of plants includes bulbs, fruit, grass, water plants, herbs, spices, houseplants, perennials, shrubs, trees, vegetables, vines, crawlers and wild flowers.

**Expert Gardener**  www.expertgardener.co.uk

Backed by British TV favourites Alan Titchmarch and Charlie Dimmock, this is an online community that puts you in touch with fellow gardening enthusiasts. The team includes garden designers, writers and nurserymen. The vibrant site hosts a chat room and news service, while its well-stocked library lets you search for gardening information.

**Gardening.com**  www.gardening.com

Want to find out what an Antirrhinum majus is, or what kind of bulbs to plant in your garden? Either way, you'll find it here. Dig into the database of over 3,000 illustrated plants for a fast and easy way to find the perfect plant for your garden.

**GardenGuides**  www.gardenguides.com

The vast range of advice sections, ranging from beneficial insects to shade gardens and winter techniques, make this is good destination when your search for help or information is exhausted elsewhere. There are flower, vegetable and herb guides and seasonal tips.

**GardenLinks UK**  www.gardenlinks.ndo.co.uk

A good place to start searching for gardening information, with comprehensive directory listings for British gardening suppliers, historic parks and gardens open to visitors.

**GardenWeb Forums**  www.gardenweb.com

One of the largest communities of gardeners on the Internet, covering more than 90 different plants, regions and topics – handily searchable from the homepage. This is the place to come to tap the collective wisdom of thousands of other gardeners.

**MySeasons.com**                    **www.gardensolutions.com**

This US-based site's plant smart service helps you find out what works and what doesn't. The care guides help you plan how you want to set up your garden, and how to keep it green and growing.

**Natural History Museum's**            **http:/fff.nhm.ac.uk/**
**Postcode Plants database**              **fff/searchPC.htm**

Only useful for British gardeners, who will be fascinated to discover what flora and fauna are native to their areas. The entire area of the UK is divided into 3259 10x10-km grid squares, with dots to indicate the presence of wild species in each one. Enter your postcode to find out which square is yours.

---

**Newsgroups**

---

**alt.garden.pond.chat** – before you get digging, talk to those who've done it before

**aus.gardens** – Aussie garden discussion

**rec.gardens** – general gardening newsgroup

**rec.gardens.orchids** – love your orchids? You are not alone

**uk.rec.gardening** – garden obsessives of the UK unite

## //GOVERNMENT

---

**The United Kingdom**

---

*It's good to see our taxes well spent. No really it is. The range and options provided by the collected sites of HM's government mean you never again can say 'I did not know.' Delve deep into the corridors of power.*

**The Army**                         **www.army.mod.uk**

Hi-tech, video-game influenced design conveys news of the army's deployments around the world and plenty of information for anyone thinking of applying – the site has details of army life, equipment and organisation. The A-Z of army regiments has links to all the regimental homepages.

**The Charity Commission**          www.charity-commission.gov.uk
Exists to give the public confidence in the integrity of charities in England and Wales. This sites hosts details of all 180,000 registered charities and publishes reviews and consultation documents online.

**Environment Agency**          www.environment-agency.gov.uk
A well-designed site that presents the latest news, government research and data about the environment. It is well geared to the non-professional user, with a useful postcode search facility making it easy to find out what's going on in your local area.

**Explore Parliament**          www.explore.parliament.uk
Aimed at kids, this is a great place to expand their parliamentary knowledge, with details of bills going through parliament, an online debating chamber and a series of taxing quizzes. The question time section answers queries submitted by email.

**Houses of Parliament**          www.parliament.uk
Despite its utilitarian design this is a superb online guide to all the workings of the House of Commons and Lords. You can use the site to read every Hansard from 1988 to the present or check what your MP is up to in the register of interests. If you're keen to go there to see democracy in action, there's also a useful guide to arranging a visit.

**Inland Revenue**          www.inlandrevenue.gov.uk
A highly functional, and on occasion indecently cheerful, site that covers everything to do with tax and National Insurance in a logical and easy-to-follow manner. Confusion-busting features include detailed help on completing the complex self-assessment form.

**Official Documents**          www.official-documents.co.uk
Still under development, this service provided by the government's own publishers, the Stationery Office, aims to help Internet users

find official publications – and perhaps save a few trees in the process.

**Open.gov.uk**                     **www.open.gov.uk**
This high-powered, easy-to-use central search engine should be your first point of call for any UK government related information. New additions are prominently flagged, so coming here is a good way to keep on top of the colossal amount of information added to the government public network every day. Search by organisation or topic.

**The Penal Lexicon**                     **www.penlex.org.uk**
This server provides information on matters concerned with prisons, criminal justice and penal affairs. The focus is on prisons in England, Wales and Northern Ireland, but as information becomes available coverage will extend to Europe and North America.

**Public Record Office**                     **www.pro.gov.uk**
The PRO stores the UK's most important government documents inside a fortress-like building in Kew, London. As well as excellent services for genealogists (covered in detail in Chapter 7), this site provides access to the latest sensitive records as they released.

**The Scottish Parliament**                     **www.scottish.parliament.uk**
A dour-looking site that nevertheless contains everything the Scottish political buff could ever wish to know, including details of all the Scottish MPs and background on the parliament's not very extensive range of powers.

**10 Downing Street**                     **www.number-10.gov.uk**
A record of the government's progress presented as popular journalism, with forums for public debate and issues made accessible – a welcome change from most of the rather dry sites in this section. Occasionally adopts a rather 'matey' presidential approach.

**The Treasury**                     **www.hm-treasury.gov.uk**
Most useful around budget time, when it gears up its service to

provide a range of tools to assist you in calculating how tax changes will affect you. Throughout the year the site hosts a huge collection of solid economic resources, including details of all budgets since 1994.

**UK State**                                    **www.ukstate.com**
User-friendly format which can really help you discover what policies impact on your life. It's quite strange to find a shopping basket on a government site, but selling HMSO's excellent range of print products is a big part of this site's mission. Just one of the many options is the opportunity to find your MP by postcode, surname, party or constituency.

**Welsh Assembly**                    **www.assembly.wales.gov.uk**
Explains how the Assembly (or Cynulliad Cenedlaethol Cymru, as they also call it) works and gives comprehensive details about your representatives in Cardiff. The policy and information area contains accessible general reference material and all those heavyweight legislative documents. There's a mirror site in Welsh.

---

**International**

---

*Whether you fancy a sneaky peak inside the Oval Office or prefer a statelier introduction to UN headquarters in New York, it seems the era of open government really has arrived. With every Western government putting their procedures online, it's easy for citizens to monitor those governing in their name.*

**Canada Site**                              **http://canada.gc.ca**
A hugely impressive starting point for access to Canadian government agencies. It acts as the Internet access point through which users can obtain information about Canada, its government and its programme.

**European Union**                          **http://europa.eu.int**
Vast portal that includes access to new releases from EU institutions, a calendar of events, the official Euro rates and all the

latest statistics. Elsewhere there's details of citizens' rights, key issues such as the Euro and employment figures, and access to the EU's huge public access databases.

## FedGov                                       www.fed.gov.au

Nicely designed entry point for all Australian Commonwealth Government authorised information and services. Has extensive introductions to the way government, parliament and the legislature works, profiles of ministers and access to all other government sites.

## FedWorld Information Network          www.fedworld.gov

Access to thousands of US Government web sites and more than half a million official documents and databases. A good place to visit if you are planning vacation or business travel, wish to review and download tax forms or consult the site's US Business Advisor.

## 4Government.com                      www.4government.com

'Of the people, by the people and for the people'. So be a good citizen and explore the Constitution, White House, cabinet departments, Congress and Supreme Court via this comprehensive set of links.

## Governments on the Web            www.gksoft.com/govt/en

Whatever official information you need, you'll find a link to it here – parliaments, ministries, law courts, embassies, consulates and more. There are also links to political parties and party alliances on national, regional and municipal levels.

## GovSpot                                   www.govspot.org

Excellent US government information portal. Find the best sites to contact your representatives, stay on top of current issues, research Supreme Court decisions, download tax forms and search government documents.

## Nato                                          www.nato.int

The latest details on Nato forces deployment, plus interesting background on the its formation, an introduction to its main policies and an informative guide to its structure and members and partners. The online library contains a complete archive of all official documents.

### South Africa Government Online                www.gov.za

With this comprehensive homepage, South Africa's government makes sure that information from all manner of local and national government bodies is accessible online. There's a comprehensive overview of, and quick links to, all the places you can find official material.

### United Nations                www.un.org

As you might expect, this is one of the biggest and most detailed sites on the entire web, presented in six different languages. The site aims to keep visitors up to date with news on the work of the United Nations High Commission for Refugees and details of UN Assembly votes. There's also lots of reference information, including the full text of the oft-quoted Universal Declaration of Human Rights.

### The White House                www.whitehouse.gov

Offers a huge range of information, but in a rather surprising home-on-the-range style quite out of kilter with the Internet revolution. The presidential biographies are particularly thorough, with links to each president's inaugural address. There's an interesting section on White House history, and details of all the executive's policy decisions.

---

### Newsgroups

---

**alt.politics.british** – sack the government, sack the opposition

**alt.politics.green** – ban the bomb, save the rainforest

**alt.politics.usa** – political issues in the US

**alt.politics.usa.constitution.gun-rights** – the right to bear arms

**alt.politics.white-power** – and some of the idiots who use them

**soc.politics.marxism** – bring back Marx and Engels

**talk.politics.china** – on second thoughts, don't

**uk.politics** – stand up and be counted

**uk.politics.electoral** – it's always election time

**wales.politics.assembly** – oh go on, please do

## //HEALTH & FITNESS

*All you need to save a life, authenticate health information or assume the lotus position. There's comprehensive medical coverage of every ailment imaginable under 'Medical Information' on page 132. This section has basic healthcare portals, so you can stay fit and healthy.*

**BBC Education – 999**     **www.bbc.co.uk/education/999/lifesaver**
BBC television's 999 tells the stories of ordinary people who find themselves in extraordinary situations. Most show how basic knowledge of first aid helped save a life. While you can't be trained completely online, this straightforward site covers the most common injuries and how to treat them.

**BBC Health**                             **www.bbc.co.uk/health**
Take advantage of this site's authoritative guides to research anything worrying you – topics covered include arthritis, back pain and hormones. One of the best sections here is the huge web guide that explains where to find the best health and fitness sites.

**The Health Centre**               **www.healthcentre.org.uk**
Guides you smoothly through the huge amount of health information available online, with about 4,500 links (mainly to UK sites, but some international sites are included too). You can get lost in here for hours.

**Health In Focus**                   **www.healthinfocus.co.uk**
This site does a good job telling you the facts about a disease, showing how you can expect to be treated, the level of medical

care you can expect and the treatments you are likely to receive. The excellent glossary clearly explains complicated medical terms.

**MyNutrition**                    www.mynutrition.co.uk
An online guide to everything to do with healthy food, eating and supplements. The Myconsultation section is a step-by-step guide to creating your own individual dietary programme.

**Quackwatch**                    www.quackwatch.com
A member of the Consumer Federation of America, this non-profit organisation aims to improve the quality of health information on the Internet. It works hard to combat health-related frauds, myths, fads, and fallacies.

**Selfcare Guide**                www.healthgate.co.uk/selfcare
Medical training for wannabe medics. This site demonstrates that with products already available, you could, for example, test yourself for HIV or use an automatic defibrillator to resuscitate someone after a heart attack.

**ThinkNatural.com**              www.thinknatural.com
This welcoming site has everything you could wish to know about vitamins, minerals, aromatherapy and homeopathy. Although the ultimate aim is to sell things, there's lots of detailed background information on what these products are said to achieve.

**Wired for Health**              www.wiredforhealth.gov.uk
Two UK government departments put their heads together and came up with this site as a way to ensure schoolchildren (and their teachers) can get health information at the touch of a button.

**The Yoga Site**                 www.yogasite.com
Discover the difference between a yogi, a guru and a swami, and determine which of yoga's many styles is best suited to you. This excellent site is also a good place to find out where to study yoga in India.

**Newsgroups**

**alt.health** – stay well

**alt.fitness.aerobic** – jump up and down, then jump around

**alt.fitness.marketplace** – buy one of those tummy strengthening things

**alt.yoga** – stretch out, chill out

**misc.fitness** – general fitness chat

## //HOLIDAY DESTINATIONS

*The Internet brings the full ranges of all the major guidebooks to your desktop, supplemented by local insights and informed comment from those in the know. Whatever your destination, have a quick search to see if it has a standalone site, although the quality of these varies wildly. You'll also find thousands of newsgroups where people swap advice and information on even the most remote and untouristed destinations.*

**The Budget Travellers Guide to**     **www3.ympatico.ca/donna.**
**Sleeping in Airports**     **smcsherry/airports.htm**
If you're planning a holiday and looking to skim just a little bit more cash off the overall cost, this idiosyncratic guide is for you. Made up of thousands of personal reports on nights spent in airports around the world, this is the definitive guide to where, and where not to sleep if you want to wake up refreshed and ready for that 12 hour long-haul flight.

**Expedia**     **www.expedia.com**
America's most popular travel destination, and an excellent place to research your trip abroad. Expedia's unrivalled size means that you can check and compare flight times and hotel accommodation for every destination in the world. For specific area information on a particular place click on the World Guide. Expedia also has mirror

sites for the UK (**www.expedia.co.uk**) and Australia (**www.expedia.com.au**).

### Fielding's DangerFinder       www.fieldingtravel.com/df

The Internet's most comprehensive guide to Earth's least visited places. Its authors boast of meetings with warlords, hijackings, stints in the French Foreign Legion and Colombian jailbreaks. For anyone determined to holiday in a war zone, the information here will help you to stay healthy, happy and alive.

### Iglu       www.iglu.com

Research and plan your winter holiday here. The huge number of accommodation options – in resorts around the world – are supplemented by 3D maps and snow reports. The site includes detailed information on destinations and road, rail and air travel to the slopes.

### Kasbah       www.kasbah.com

This, the world's largest specialist travel search engine, lets you search 150,000 hand-picked travel sites from 230 countries. Usefully, your search returns are sorted into categories including culture and history as well as the usual accommodation and transport. The site's makers seem to think that Canadians, Aussies and Kiwis have particularly unusual travel needs, so they have provided special sections especially for them.

### Lonely Planet       www.lonelyplanet.com

Backpackers' bible goes digital, with concise but useful starting information on all their destinations. You can also get the latest news from travellers who are still on the road – without having to listen to them drawling on in some grubby hostel or hippy café.

### Minding Your Health Abroad       www.masta.org

Covering such worries as contaminated water, suspect seafood and rabies infected animals, this is an authoritative guide to immunisations and diseases that clearly explains the risks and any jabs you may require.

**Rough Guides**       http://travel.roughguides.com

Explore more than 14,000 destinations on this award-winning travel site from these well-known travel publishers. Offers up-to-the-minute details and illuminating commentary on thousands of destinations and travel issues. Country and regional guides include in-depth site information, listings, colour photographs and maps.

**Time Out**       www.timeout.com

What's hot in all the major cities of the world. The bright and insightful advice on each is divided into ten sections: Living Guide, Accommodation, Sightseeing, Essential Information, Entertainment, Eating and Drinking, Shopping, Kids, Gay and Lesbian, and Web links.

**Travel Advice**       www.fco.gov.uk/travel

Aimed primarily at British citizens travelling abroad, there's plenty of useful advice here about health and personal safety. You can access the full range of the Foreign Office's Travel Advice notices, and get embassy and consulate location details. Similar services are provided by the US and Australian governments at http://travel.state.gov/travel_warnings.html and www.dfat.gov.au respectively.

**Travel.com.au**       www.travel.com.au

Half the fun of a trip is the planning. This is a brilliant one-stop shop that lets you check out all the alternatives. Research your destination, use the Trip Planner to build your own holiday experience, or tap into the advice offered by the site's passionate travel specialists.

**Travelocity.com**       www.travelocity.com

A truly global travel site, Travelocity is beginning to look almost exactly like Excite (or is it the other way around?). They offer the same huge range of features too. Here you can find and price cars, hotels, airline tickets and cruises, or even choose your own airline seat online.

**World Wide Gazetteer**                    www.c-allen.dircon.co.uk
Hand-picked selection of travel destinations that gives you the chance to consult tourist information, do a little research into local history, and read the local papers or get the latest weather or exchange rates.

**WorldTravelGuide.Net**                    www.wtgonline.com
The travel professionals' favourite, and one of the most comprehensive and objective guides to countries. Click on your destination, and you'll get a brief overview, with the option of accessing far more details if required. It's all presented in a detailed and highly structured way.

---

**Newsgroups**

---

**rec.travel.africa** – from Cape Town to Cairo

**rec.travel.asia** – from Karachi to Katmandu

**rec.travel.australia+nz** – from Perth to Wellington

**rec.travel.latin-america** – from Tijuana to Tierra del Fuego

**rec.travel.usa-canada** – from Anchorage to the Keys

## //HOUSE BUYING

*Buying or selling a home is one of life's most stressful experiences. Thankfully a whole host of online services have sprung up to take the hassle out of moving, and there are sites that let you browse property lists, sort out financing and arrange surveys from your computer.*

**Bamboo Avenue**                    www.bambooavenue.com
An excellent destination for independent help and advice on every aspect of buying or selling a property. Whether you request a quote for a moving related service, or need some independent advice you will be allocated a real live Moving Buddy to guide you through the process.

**Consumer Real Estate Center**   www.realestate.com
As well as lots of advice on buying and selling, this is a good place to search for agents and US homes, evaluate property, get financing and organise the entire process. You can find out what your home is worth now – and what it might be worth in the future – with the site's free residential property report.

**HomeBuilder.com**   www.homebuilder.com
Allows potential homebuyers to browse, free of charge, through America's biggest searchable database of new homes. You can email the builder with detailed requests for information and use the site's search facility to hunt by geographic location within a given state, specifying individual home details such as price, square footage and number of bedrooms and bathrooms.

**Homemovers**   www.homemovers.co.uk
One of the largest selections of properties for sale in the UK, with about 220,000 houses in all areas and price brackets. Beats trudging round the estate agents.

**Homepages**   www.homepages.co.uk
Another service with a database to search for properties that meet your specific needs. You can then look at a map of the area and find local schools. The email notification service lets you know when they've found a property that matches your requirements.

**HouseWeb**   www.houseweb.co.uk
Hundreds of pages of independent advice, information, resources and tips for the home-seeker from a portal that lets you access over 150,000 properties. You'll also find the latest mortgage rates and property market analysis.

**International Real Estate Digest**   www.ired.com
Excellent site with 30,000 reviewed links to property-related web sites throughout the world. As useful for real estate professionals – including surveyors, inspectors, brokers and sales people – as for buyers and sellers.

**Mooov**                                 **www.mooov.com**
Although the site claims the Internet's biggest UK property database (with at least 250,000 properties) it has much more to offer. If you're not sure about the precise location you want to move into, a handy 3-stage diagnostic tool lets you search for areas that closely match your circumstances.

**MoneyWorld**                     **www.moneyworld.co.uk/homebuying**
Lots of help for homebuyers, with news, features, guides, contact phone numbers and links and a mortgage finder. There are excellent guides to buying and selling, legal issues and a whole range of mortgages and a useful home insurance calculator to help you work out how much cover you need.

**Mortgage Information**        **www.moneyextra.co.uk/mortgages**
Need a mortgage or re-mortgage? Hunting for the best deal? This site lets you compare mortgages from 120 lenders. Rates are updated constantly and you can search according to your own specific criteria. There is also an excellent A-Z glossary of mortgages.

**PropertyLive**                          **www.propertylive.co.uk**
Search for properties to buy and rent throughout the UK. To speed the process up you can specify what facilities the property should have. You can then contact estate agencies for more details and sign up to suitable agency mailing lists.

**Really Moving**                         **www.reallymoving.com**
Excellent resource providing practical advice and help in finding surveyors, removal companies and more. Fill in your details and the site provides instant quotes for any removals related service you require. The handy planning and reminder service makes sure nothing important is overlooked – you can even order change-of-address cards.

**alt.buildings.insurance** – sort out some insurance for your new home

**alt.business.property** – the buying and selling of property

**alt.invest.real-estate** – where to buy

**alt.real.estate-agents** – where to get help buying

**alt.real-estate-aus** – where to get help buying down under

## //INSURANCE

*If you've found yourself in despair at the confusing variety of insurance options, you'll be relieved to hear that the Internet makes finding the best policy much easier. The best thing is that you can get instant quotes from a number of different insurers, all keen to win your custom.*

**The Association of**      **www.abi.org.uk/consumer2/**
**British Insurers**      **consumer.htm**
Useful advice for consumers, from an authoritative source, covering a huge range of insurance issues. Explanatory sections demystify a gaggle of topics, including motor, household, travel, medical, life insurance and pensions.

**Insurance UK**      **www.insuranceuk.net**
The quick quote facility enables you to search the site's directory of intermediaries for the type of insurance you want. The site then displays a list of brokers who match your needs, and supplies handy links.

**Insure.com**      **www.insure.com**
By combining the reporting style of a daily newspaper with a wealth of insurance advice, this site has become one of America's most popular consumer websites. There's unbiased reporting on the insurance industry and all the background information you

could need. Best of all, the site is truly independent – it doesn't sell insurance itself, so it can afford to be impartial.

**LineOne**                                      **www.lineone.net/clubs/**
**insurance guide**                               **money/insurance**

Although it's hidden away in this ISP's content pages, this site is well worth a visit for the clear, basic insurance information. Household, travel, motor and even pet insurance are clearly explained here. You can get a quote for reasonably priced life insurance, check out LineOne's best buys, or find recommended life insurers on the web.

**Screentrade**                                   **www.screentrade.com**

Helps you research the right deal on your motor, home and travel insurance. After you've indicated your requirements, the site can prepare a selection of competitive, personalised quotes in just a few moments. You can then compare prices and cover, and thus see exactly what you're getting for your money.

## //INVESTING

*The Internet is rapidly replacing traditional sources of financial information, and is revolutionising the relationship between investor and broker, as trading sites win customers and reputations. Now anyone can have access to data previously only available to the professionals, such as high quality charts, stock tickers, company quarterly reports, earnings estimates, trader and analyst recommendations.*

**E*TRADE UK**                                    **www.etrade.co.uk**

Free membership gives you access to 15 minute delayed quotes from the London Stock Exchange, news headlines, company information and your personalised stockwatch list. Lets you research the past, present, and predicted future of a company.

**Financial Services Authority**                  **www.fsa.gov.uk/**
**Consumer Help**                                 **consumer**

The guys who regulate the UK financial services industry provide a splendid source of information about financial advice in the UK. There's advice on getting the best deal, consumer help and frequently asked financial questions. Nicely illustrated and easy to use.

### Financial Times                    www.ft.com

This is an essential stop for anyone wanting to make money on the stockmarket. The tremendous size and range of the site, backed by the authority of its sister paper, make this the best place to begin your research into a potential investment. If you can't find it here, it probably isn't worth looking for in the first place.

### Interactive Investor International          www.iii.co.uk

Excellent UK site with price information and a wide-ranging directory of financial services. Some of the most comprehensive investing information available is smoothly coupled with online tools that make it easy to keep track of your investments. Beware of people talking up static shares on the bulletin boards.

### Market-Eye Internet                 www.marketeye.co.uk

Offers excellent coverage of the UK markets, with professional level data, tools and research. The service uses the same displays and sources that dealers and traders have on their screens.

### MoneyWorld Investment   www.moneyworld.co.uk/investment

If you're looking to check the past performance of investment funds such as unit trusts, you'll find extensive listings here. The site's 'PowerSearches' are a useful way of analysing investment data without any hassles. Use the Online Trading Centre to decide which broker is right for you.

### The Motley Fool                      www.fool.com

This famous site has no investment product to sell, and derives no income from your investment activities – it is a pure research facility. What you get are brilliant, personal recommendations that give the low-down on investment strategy and on any company on the market. Brits should go to their localised version at **www.fool.co.uk**.

**Sharepeople.com**                    **www.sharepeople.com**

Pulling together a colossal range of data, letting you research over 12,000 UK and International securities and unit trusts. Access comprehensive company data, news and research, brokers' forecasts and price charts, and use the portfolio management tools to make sure your investments are performing well.

**TheStreet.co.uk**                    **www.thestreet.co.uk**

British version of the runaway Wall Street success story (at **www.thestreet.com**), offering a similar formula of breaking news, expert commentary and 'Investor Basics,' to improve investors' knowledge. And knowledge is power.

---

**Newsgroups**

**alt.invest.market-crash** – how to spot a crash, and where to get off

**aus.invest** – where to put your Australian dollars

**misc.invest.futures** – long-term bets

**misc.invest.marketplace** – trade shares on the Usenet

**misc.invest.stocks** – hot, inside tips

## //JOBS

*Looking for a new job has never been easier, with companies increasingly using the Internet as a vital part of their recruiting process. It's easy to search for jobs that meet your own criteria, a real contrast from the day's when you scoured newspaper recruitment sections hoping to come across a suitable post.*

**Canadajobs.com**                    **www.canadajobs.com**

This site collects all the sites that have job listings in Canada in one place. Has loads of links to job databases, government job banks, employment agencies, and Canadian companies that have job listings on their own websites.

**Career Solutions**     **www.careersolutions.co.uk**

Lots of free career guidance, which you can access through the Route Planner sign on the homepage. As well as a useful introduction to job hunting on the web, you'll find advice here on getting a satisfying, challenging job, and on what to do if you're sacked or made redundant.

**Careerpath.com**     **www.careerpath.com**

Provides an aggregated selection of current jobs listings, which come from two sources: the Help Wanted ads of America's leading newspapers, and the websites of leading employers. No listing remains on the database for more than two weeks, so the vacancies are very up-to-date.

**Careers.com**     **www.careers.com**

Hardly the best-looking of sites, but it's versatile and it works well. And more than 4 million job-seekers check in every month, making it the most popular job site in the US. There are a huge range of options to help you find a job online.

**Careers Information and**    **www.aiuto.net/**
**Guidance on the Web**      **uk.htm**

Useful guide to more than 400 UK sites dedicated to job searching, professions, vocational training and universities. Nicely organised, it makes an excellent access point for careers information and guidance on the net.

**GisaJob**     **www.gisajob.com**

This was one of the first free recruitment websites in the UK, and it's still one of the biggest. A recent survey claimed that 8 out of 10 candidates who had submitted their CVs to GisaJob said they had received a good or excellent response from agencies.

**I-resign**     **www.i-resign.com**

Provides a wicked spin on the standard job site, with information and advice for anyone recently resigned or about to take the plunge. The site gives tips on how to deal with the whole process, from making the decision in the first place to leaving your company on the right note.

**JobBankUSA**                                    www.jobbankusa.com

This is where to come if you've got a big job interview, and need to do some serious research into the company you're hoping to join. There are links to industry associations, and lots of news on individual companies. If you get the job, come back to assess your potential earnings and take advantage of the handy relocation tools.

**Job-Hunt**                                        www.job-hunt.org

An extremely large, but nevertheless usable, index of online resources for job hunters, organised into logical categories to help you find the resources you need. Search through job openings, post your résumé, get advice on job seeking and career changing, and research potential employers.

**JobSearch**                                      www.jobsearch.co.uk

Find contact details, job descriptions and salary information online at this very useful site. There is an excellent, comprehensive guide to preparing professional CVs and résumés. The vacancy list is constantly updated, so each time you perform a search, you should be looking at up-to-the-minute jobs.

**JobSite**                                         www.jobsite.co.uk

Created in 1995 this is a long-running Internet recruitment platform that claims to attract hundreds of thousands of candidates every month. Search Europe's leading jobs, or register to receive information on new vacancies by email. With more than 100,000 jobs advertised a month from 35 industries, there's a good chance you'll find something here.

**Jobs Unlimited**                                 www.jobsunlimited.co.uk

Combining the tailored job listings of the UK *Guardian* newspaper, this site also has useful advice on interview techniques and CV writing. If you can't find a recent advert, contact the site with the date you saw it and they will send you a copy.

**Links to the World of Opportunities**  
www.welcomeindia.com/jobs

On first glance you might wonder what this site has going for it. Isn't it just a page of links? Well yes – but what links. Someone has spent weeks compiling an enormous range of job sites in the US, UK, Canada, Australia and New Zealand. And while we're here, the main site at **www.welcomeindia** is an excellent gateway to the Indian subcontinent.

**Monster**  
www.monster.co.uk

Monster.com is America's most successful job site. This UK version offers broadly similar services, including a career-management account in which you store five different CVs and covering letters, track your online applications and get sent email when a job listing matches your criteria.

**NetJobs.co.uk**  
www.netjobs.co.uk

Useful extras make this, one of the UK's fastest-growing job sites, a good place to research job hunting before you commit yourself. You get the usual online advice, CV tips and advice on how to perform in your job interview.

**StepStone**  
www.stepstone.co.uk

Claiming to be the leading European Internet recruitment site, this has one of the largest employment databases on the net. They currently offer more than 70,000 job vacancies and attract more than 1.9 million visitors every month.

**Top Jobs on the Net**  
www.topjobs.net

Good for management, professional and technical jobs. There are also hints on how to manage your career and make the right impression at an interview. Before you start looking, you can do some psychometric tests to determine whether you are happy in your work. There's an Australian version at **www.topjobs.com.au**.

**Totaljobs**  
www.totaljobs.com

Find out whether you are being paid enough with this site's handy salary checker. Usefully, you can research jobs by specific region and ask details of relevant jobs to be sent direct to your email address.

**Working and**          **www.travelnotes.org/**
**studying abroad**          **Travel/working_abroad.htm**
Finding employment abroad is harder than at home, because you generally don't have the contacts. This is an excellent place to start if you are determined to work your way around the world. And one of the messages here is that you'll need to be, or you won't get anywhere.

---

### Newsgroups

**alt.jobs.gigs.offered** – out-of-work musicians welcome

**aus.ads.jobs** – jobs going everywhere from Darwin to Tasmania

**uk.jobs.contract** – short-term work opportunities

**uk.jobs.offered** – list of available jobs, needing to be matched with ...

**uk.jobs.wanted** – ... people looking for jobs

## //LANGUAGES

*Whether you want to learn a language, translate a document or just pick your way through the minefield of high-tech buzzwords, the Internet can help.*

**alt.culture**          **www.altculture.com**
Do you find yourself left behind by the complex terminology and slang used by the kind of people who wear plastic trousers and wave their Palm Pilots around? This site keeps a handle on subcultures in all their diversity, covering everything from grunge, gangsta and trip-hop to cyberpunk, extreme sports and political correctness.

**Babelfish** http://babelfish.altavista.digital.com

Named after the universal language-translating organism in *The Hitchhiker's Guide to the Galaxy*, this free service converts words, phrases or documents of up to five kilobytes – about 1,000 characters – from one European language to another. The results can be pretty rough, but you can usually get the gist of the translated document.

**Foreign Languages for Travellers** www.travlang.com/languages

Help for anyone else interested in learning a foreign tongue. Choose the language you want to learn by clicking on its national flag.

**FreeTranslation.com** www.freetranslation.com

A good site for rapid translations of foreign language text and web pages. Each translation can be up to five pages of text. Like Babelfish (above), the results can be quirky but the general meaning shines through. The service is fast and free.

**HandSpeak** www.handspeak.com

This is an excellent introduction to sign languages, also beneficial for self-tutoring. Although it focuses on the American Sign Language, there are guides to all the major international languages. The site helps deaf children and deaf adults to learn vocabulary.

**The Human-Languages Page** www.june29.com/HLP

This is a comprehensive catalogue of language-related Internet resources. Online language lessons, translating dictionaries, native literature, translation services, language schools, or just a little information on a language you've heard about: the HLP probably has something to suit your needs.

**Online Dictionaries and** http://rivendel.com/~
**Translators** ric/resources/dictionary.html

Comprehensive site that has attempted to put as many online multi-lingual dictionaries at your disposal as possible. They prefer sites that have a searchable index. Some may require your browser to have the ability to read the language being translated to.

**The Rap Dictionary**                                    **www.rapdict.org**
In September 1992, when the umpteenth question on the meaning of a Public Enemy lyric was posted to the alt.rap newsgroup, Patrick 'Tricky' Atoon decided to silence the questions once and for all by posting a list of rap definitions on a regular basis. Parental guidance definitely necessary.

**The Slang Dictionary**                          **www.peevish.co.uk/slang**
Language is in constant evolution, especially in a country with as many regional dialects as the UK – and lively slang is the sign of a healthy, living language. It's well documented here. Inevitably, much of the contents focus on bodily functions rarely discussed in polite circles, so readers of a sensitive disposition should beware.

---

**Newsgroups**

---

**alt.usage.english** – howe too yuse corectly yor Englis

**soc.culture.french** – bonjour, my foreign friends

**soc.culture.german** – don't mention the war

**uk.culture.language** – the linguistic melting pot of multi-cultural Britain

## //LEGAL RIGHTS

*The legal world can seem impenetrable and expensive – no surprise then, that most people would rather do anything than consult a lawyer. The Internet is proving a breath of fresh air through the profession. Whether you want to find a way out of your marriage (you can now arrange a divorce online) or are looking for legal assistance, the net makes it easy.*

**Advice Guide**                                   **www.adviceguide.org.uk**
Well-organised site with basic information on your legal rights.

Advice is free, confidential and impartial and covers a huge range of subjects, including debt, benefits, housing, legal matters, employment, immigration and consumer issues. If your problem is complicated, the site suggests you get in touch with your local Citizens Advice Bureau – and explains how to do so.

### DesktopLawyer                                www.desktoplawyer.co.uk

Offering a broad range of content designed to help cope with everyday legal problems, you'll find guidance not only on specific legal issues such as wills, divorce, employment and court matters, but also tips on more general matters like tax, relationships, schools and finance.

### FindLaw                                            www.findlaw.com

Offers a vast array of information on areas such as family law, estate planning, and consumer credit. The site bears more than a passing resemblance to Yahoo, which makes it easy to find your way around, despite the mass of options.

### FreeAdvice.com                                  www.freeadvice.com

The exhaustive legal content here has been principally prepared by leading attorneys from over 25 leading American law firms, from the East Coast to Hawaii. They provide a wealth of answers to 3,000 of the most commonly asked legal questions. This site is easy to navigate, covering everything from aviation law to tax, and if you can't find what you need, you can pose questions to online lawyers.

### ItsOfficial.net                                    www.itsofficial.net

Britons: do you want to know how a law is made? Do Bills start in the House of Commons or House of Lords? What is the Committee Stage? What does Royal Assent mean? All the processes that go into creating a piece of legislation, clearly explained.

### JustAsk                                            www.justask.org.uk

Need information on a legal problem? Want to know who and where your local adviser is? How much will it cost, and can you get financial help? This is an excellent source of legal help – covering England and Wales – from the Community Legal Service.

### Lawrights    www.lawrights.co.uk

Providing expert advice on everything from adoption to injunctions, this site makes a valuable first port of call for anyone with pressing legal problems. Even if you don't find the information you need, swotting up here will stand you in good stead when it comes to employing a lawyer.

### Nolo.com    www.nolo.com

Whether you want to clean up your credit or form a corporation, this site has hundreds of answers to your legal questions. The A-Z index of legal topics covers everything from automobiles to wills. If you still can't find the help you need, you can ask Auntie Nolo.

### Solicitors and Legal Resources in the UK    www.venables.co.uk

This excellent portal, links to the main legal sites in the UK and Ireland, as well as registers of solicitors and barristers on the web. Information is organised by topic, and includes accidents, benefits, conveyancing, employment, housing, patents, tax and wills.

### UK LegalResource    www.uklegal.com

A nationwide service that helps locate barristers, solicitors, private investigators and legal experts. You'll find it easier to track down these people here than through a search engine.

---

### Newsgroups

---

**alt.censorship** – what they don't want you to know

**alt.lawyers.sue.sue.sue** – sue, and friends, criticise the US legal system

**alt.uk.law** – UK law chat

**misc.legal** – general legal discussion

**uk.legal** – more views from the bench

# //LITERATURE

*Once a book's copyright runs out it (usually 75 years after the author's death), the book can be legally copied and displayed in full by any website that wants to. So you can download the complete text of a huge range of classic novels, plays and poems. If you're thinking of grabbing the collected works of Dickens, make sure you have enough disk space.*

**Bartleby.com**　　　　　　　　　　　**www.bartleby.com**
The pre-eminent Internet publisher of literature offers almost unlimited access to out-of-copyright books on the web. Publishes the classics of literature, non-fiction, and reference free of charge for the home, classroom, and desktop of every Internet user.

**Charles Dickens Page**　　　　**www.fidnet.com/~dap1955/dickens**
Gives an absorbing overview of Dickens's life and work, with a timeline of his life, a glimpse of Victorian England and background on the original illustrators of his novels. Don't miss the glossary of deliciously named characters such as Bumble, Sweedlepipe and Honeythunder.

**The English Server**　　　　　　　　**www.eserver.org**
Search here for a wide variety of literature, including text archives of both prose, poetry and fiction, hosted both on-site and elsewhere on the Internet.

**The Internet Classics Archive**　　　**http://classics.mit.edu**
Select from more than 400 works of classical literature, all with English translations, by 59 different authors. You can search by work and author or look for keywords in the texts themselves. There's also commentary from other users of the site, and 'reader's choice' web links.

**London Review of Books**　　　　　　**www.lrb.co.uk**
Nicely designed destination from the UK's premier literary magazine. The LRB gives its contributors the space and freedom to develop their ideas at length and in depth. The site reflects this

mission, with back issues, anthologies and indexes all available in the archive.

**New York Review of Books**                    www.nybooks.com/nyrev
Seriously good. The *New York Review of Books* has long been 'the premier literary-intellectual magazine in the English language', as *Esquire* magazine described it. You may not be able to tell a book by its cover – but you can by the buzz here. The online version adds a text archive and audio clips from a variety of distinguished literary contributors.

**Times Literary Supplement**                    www.the-tls.co.uk
The TLS covers every subject in all the world's leading languages: fiction, poetry, history, politics, philosophy, travel, medicine, archaeology, sports, classics, music, psychology. Some of the best writers in their fields discuss in depth some 2,500 books, plays, films and exhibitions. Subscribers can search back issues here.

---

## Newsgroups

---

**alt.literacy** – good grammar and spelling

**alt.writing** – bring out that best-seller

**humanities.lit.authors.shakespeare** – discuss the bard

**misc.writing** – general writing tips

**uk.culture.arts.writing** – UK writers support group

## //MAPS

*The Internet's good at geography. It can help you establish the distance as the crow flies or pinpoint your location from space. You can create and download free maps or browse ancient cartographic collections, determine the distance between key towns or plan a road trip to perfection. All the maps you could possibly need are here, somewhere.*

**Atlapedia.com**                                              www.atlapedia.com
Full colour physical and political maps as well as key facts and statistics for every country of the world. Geography, climate, people, religion, language, history and economics.

**Cybergeography**                                        www.cybergeography.com
The right place for a cybermap – a map of the Internet itself, bringing to life the electronic traffic movements beyond your computer screen. Find out about the hidden digital landscapes driving the global communications revolution. Or simply discover exactly how your email reaches Auntie Ethel.

**EmulateMe.com**                                            www.emulateme.com
One of the Internet's best sources of country data, this site also has a decent flag database and a comprehensive list of national anthems – with sound files, so you can actually hear what they're like.

**Encarta Online Atlas**                                      http://encarta.com
Follow the links to spectacular, informative portraits of all the countries of the world, with links to articles about your selected spot. The site's 360-degree views are stunning panoramas of some of the world's most beautiful and interesting locations.

**Expedia**                                              http://maps.expedia.com
One of the biggest travel portals on the Internet brings you detailed street maps of the United States and road maps of Canada, Mexico and Europe. You can save maps on the site in order to consult them later.

**Geographic Information Systems**                        http://gis.about.com
A fascinating About.com guide to GIS – the system that records, analyses and maps data about the planet for all kinds of practical uses. Emergency planners use it to calculate response times in the event of natural disasters, and it helps environmentalists to highlight land in need of protection.

**How far is it?**  www.indo.com/cgi-bin/dist

This service uses data from the US Census and a supplementary list of cities around the world to find the latitude and longitude of two places, and then calculates the distance between them as the crow flies. It also provides a map showing the two places.

**MapBlast!**  www.mapblast.com

An award-winning website that provides users with accurate maps and driving directions, as well as extensive information on services and products near your address or travel route. Also provides lodging information and reservation options, traffic reports and indicates local points of interest.

**Map**  http://plasma.nationalgeographic.
**Machine**  com/mapmachine

Fantastic site. Create your own customised maps on the fly. Just try it.

**Maps.com**  www.maps.com

This commercially orientated site has a huge variety of maps on offer, although the prices, aimed at professional users, aren't cheap. You can order political maps of the world, customised for the web and multimedia use, antique maps and satellite images.

**Maps of the Solar System**  http://maps.jpl.nasa.gov

A stunning spyglass on the cosmos. This image-packed database, supported by NASA, provides different maps of the Earth's neighbours. Select your planetary system of choice and download maps, or browse the surface features of your favourite planet or satellite.

**MapQuest**  www.mapquest.com

Perhaps the most highly-rated and popular mapping service on the web, offering users the chance to find over three million locations worldwide. They can obtain driving directions, overlay places of interest, and create and save personalised maps.

**Maps Worldwide**  www.mapsworldwide.com

Specialises in supplying maps, atlases, travel guides, satellite images, nautical charts and phrase books for the international traveller. If you're having trouble obtaining a map before you go on a holiday or business trip, this is the site for you.

**MetaSubway**  http://pavel.physics.sunysb.edu/
RR/metasubway/index-old.html

Underground, metros, subways, U-bahns, trams. Whatever rolls over rails around town, this site will have the latest maps and timetables. It's not the easiest website to navigate, but you can't fault this attempt to comprehensively list every mass-transit system in the world.

**Multimap**  www.multimap.com

Click on the UK outline map to start browsing, or enter the name of a British city, town or village, street name (London only) or postcode to get a detailed map. You can zoom in on any part by clicking on the area you wish to see.

**Perry-Castaneda Library**  www.lib.utexas.edu/
**Map Collection**  Libs/PCL/Map_collection

Browse more than 2,400 maps online. This easily accessible online collection consists of a huge selection of political, road, topographical and thematic maps for continents, oceans, world regions and foreign countries.

**Streetmap.co.uk**  www.streetmap.co.uk

Provides address searching and street map facilities for the UK. Currently there are maps for Greater London and road atlas maps for the whole of mainland Britain. You can search by Ordnance Survey grid reference or by latitude or longitude.

**TerraServer**  www.terraserver.microsoft.com

Declassified satellite images, mainly from Cold War era Soviet spy satellites. You can begin your search miles above the planet and progressively click your way down to street level. View famous places, natural landmarks, or try to find your home.

## //MEDICAL INFORMATION

*The Internet gives you free access to a phenomenal range of material that until recently would only have been available to students in the best-stocked medical libraries of a university or teaching hospital. You can easily find more detailed information than your own doctor could ever be expected to provide. You might be able to diagnose yourself, but above all you can be far better informed when discussing important medical issues with specialists. None of these sites can take the place of advice from health professionals, so always consult your doctor if you're feeling ill.*

### Aching Feet Online                    www.achingfeet.co.uk
The foot is a highly complex collection of bones, tendons and muscle that moves the entire weight of the body. If you suffer from hard corns, bunions, cramps and spasms, then this site will explain how you can get help.

### Back Pain                              www.backpain.org
UK site that aims to prevent or at least manage back pain, providing advice, support and research into appropriate treatments. Lots of advice and help for sufferers, carers and therapists.

### British Association of Plastic Surgeons    www.baps.co.uk
Sets out to demystify plastic surgery by explaining how surgeons restore form and function to damaged body parts through reconstructive surgery. One common misconception is that 'plastic' surgery is synonymous with 'cosmetic' surgery; the site reveals that cosmetic cases represent only 15 per cent of the average plastic surgeon's workload.

### The British Heart Foundation            www.bhf.org.uk
This vibrant-looking site provides access to BHF research into the causes, prevention, diagnosis and treatment of heart disease. Come here to learn emergency life support skills and find out all about heart disease, its prevention and treatment.

**CancerBACUP**                     www.cancerbacup.org.uk
With more than 2,000 pages of information this site aims to help people live with cancer by providing information and emotional support for patients, their families and professionals. Recognised as the foremost provider of cancer information in the UK.

**Contact a Family**                     www.cafamily.org.uk
Every day over 60 children in the UK are born or diagnosed with a serious disability – and this site provides support and advice to concerned parents. There is factual background on over 1,000 rare syndromes and disorders and help for families wanting to share their experiences with others.

**CyberDocs**                     www.cyberdocs.com
US-trained and -certified physicians available in various specialities, depending on your geographic location. For $50 to $75, you can schedule virtual appointments, discussing your symptoms and receiving advice through keyboard chats or videoconferencing.

**Dentanet**                     www.dentanet.org.uk
An easy-to-navigate gateway to oral health. Includes the UK's largest online directory of dentists, tons of advice about keeping your teeth and gums in good nick, and links to other oral health sites from around the world.

**Diagnostic Procedures**                     www.healthgate.co.uk/dp
Written by practising physicians, this site has details of 294 common and less common medical procedures, making it a handy quick reference site for professionals and patients alike.

**drkoop.com**                     www.drkoop.com
Set up by former US Surgeon General Dr Everett Koop, this is a patient-focused site that provides you with healthcare information on a broad variety of subjects, and access to medical news, databases, publications and communities. Follow the links to **www.drkoop.com/conditions/ency** if you want to know more about a health topic, symptom or condition. A very useful site for staying healthy.

**eMedicine**  www.emedicine.com
The collected wisdom of over 6,000 physicians makes up this huge site with online textbooks for surgery and medicine, dermatology, ophthalmology, neurology, paediatrics and veterinary medicine. Tap into the knowledge of the professionals.

**Family Medicine**  http://familymedicine.
**from About.com**  about.com
Up to 20 per cent of adults suffer from Irritable Bowel Syndrome – are you one of them? Learn how to treat IBS and other common ailments on this endlessly useful About.com site, which also covers hundreds of other topics, including allergies, bronchitis, chicken pox, food poisoning, heartburn, meningitis and strep throat.

**HealthAtoZ**  www.healthatoz.com
A comprehensive medical site developed by healthcare professionals. It provides free access to health information and lets you search a vast directory of health and medical Internet sites, all of which have been individually reviewed and rated.

**Healthfinder**  www.healthfinder.gov
A free gateway to reliable consumer health information from the US Department of Health. Leads you to selected online publications, databases and support groups, as well as government agencies that produce reliable information for the public.

**HealthGate**  http://bewell.com
A premier source of credible medical information for professionals and patients. Includes the latest research from the world's top medical journals, summarised in language that everyone can understand.

**Health In Focus**  www.healthinfocus.co.uk
The webmaster here believes that demystifying medical care and treatment options is to everyone's benefit, so this site is designed to be used as much by those who know little about a disease as by doctors researching the latest clinical developments.

**The Home Doctor**     www.medetail.co.uk/home-doc
Use this site to browse an A-Z list of symptoms to help establish what is wrong with you and pinpoint appropriate medicines before you go to the pharmacist.

**Medical Links**     www.lifestyle.co.uk/acd.htm
Comprehensive list of online medical sites. Pages are well organised and all links seems to be live, but with so many options it is easy to get sidetracked. All the registered care and nursing homes in the UK are here – and so is information on every aspect of diseases such as multiple sclerosis.

**Medicdirect**     www.medicdirect.co.uk
Hosted by leading British consultants in the UK, this site carries advice by experts in their particular field. Includes tips on self-examination, what to expect when you're having an operation and an A-Z of the most common diseases.

**Mediconsult**     http://mediconsult.com
Very popular US source of medical information. Provides exhaustive coverage of every condition imaginable, from acid reflux to vision care. There is also an extensive directory of drugs, and chat boards where you can discuss your problems with others.

**MedicineNet**     www.medicinenet.com
Network of US certified physician writers and scientists providing relevant, in-depth medical information for patients via a user-friendly website. Phantom limb pain and an analysis of gene therapy are just a few of the topics covered.

**Moorfields Eye Hospital**     www.moorfields.org.uk
Image-heavy home page eventually loads to reveal a very useful selection of material from one of the world's leading eye hospitals.

**NetDoctor.co.uk**     www.netdoctor.co.uk
Use the 'test yourself' section and consult well-known professionals like UK television doctor Hilary Jones for online

assistance. There is also regularly updated information on diseases and their treatments, and health advice for common problems.

**NHS Direct**                                   **www.nhsdirect.nhs.uk**
Britain's National Health Service provides superb material grouped into seven sections, including a healthy living guide and an A-Z guide to the NHS. The site aims to help people decide on a course of action, which could mean a trip to the pharmacist, doctor or dentist.

**The National Kidney Research Association**     **www.nkrf.org.uk**
The UK NKRA works to achieve greater knowledge of the kidney and urinary tract and the diseases that affect them. You can access their in-depth research here, but there's also general information about kidney disease and the needs of sufferers.

**Natural Remedies**                             **www.pathlights.com/**
**Encyclopedia**                                 **nr_encyclopedia**
From the homepage click on a subject you are interested in, and it will take you to a more detailed disease index. There's a wealth of information on each one, and details of alternative remedies for those who wish to avoid conventional medicine.

**Official Mad Cow Disease Homepage**            **www.mad-cow.org**
Put that hamburger down – now! This site has more than 6000 articles on bovine spongiform encephalopathy, Creutzfeldt-Jakob disease (CJD), prions, scrapie and other mysterious and incurable brain diseases. Frustratingly, there is no obvious way to search.

**Patient UK**                                   **www.patient.co.uk**
Pleasingly simple UK directory, aiming to help non-medical people find information on health and illness. Includes links to hundreds of UK health sites, and some overseas sites too.

**Planet Medica**                                **www.planetmedica.co.uk**
Excellent site that presents ways to assess your health and measure the severity of your symptoms before calling the doctor. You can also compare your general health with average health standards.

**QuitSmokingSupport.com**      http://anyboard.net/
health/quitsmoking

A good place to discuss giving up the evil weed and to share your experiences. By posting your questions or comments here you can help others who want to stub out their bad habits.

**The SurgeryDoor**      www.surgerydoor.co.uk

Site that says it aims to provide the most comprehensive and useful online health service in Britain. There is some good stuff here, but the emphasis on selling makes it clear that this is an e-commerce business, and not just a virtual surgery.

**US National Library of Medicine**      www.nlm.nih.gov

Funded by the US taxpayer, this is the largest online medical resource in the world. Until recently high access charges made it very expensive, but it's now mostly free, and fields more than 250,000 enquiries each day.

**UKHealthNet**      www.24dr.com

Slip these British family doctors a tenner and they will respond personally to your questions. The process may take a few days. For £15, a GP will respond by live audio or video.

**WebMD**      www.webmd.com

This excellent US site is an independent daily health and medical news service that has won a reputation for providing the latest information to the general public, patients, physicians, nurses, and other health care professionals. Well worth a look.

---

**Newsgroups**

---

**alt.infertility.pregnancy** – alternative strategies

**alt.med.allergy** – hay fever suffers of the world unite

**alt.support.arthritis** – support and advice

**alt.support.depression** – let yourself be cheered up

**misc.health.diabetes** – lots of good advice

**sci.med** – general medical discussion

**sci.med.dentistry** – teeth tales

**sci.med.diseases.cancer** – vast information source

**sci.med.pharmacy** – drugs for chemists

**talk.politics.medicine** – the ethics of medicine

## //MOVIES

*If you are one of those people who loves to know every little tiny detail of a movie, and will go to the cinema countless times to make sure you don't miss anything, then the Internet is a godsend. It brings fans from around the world together to share their passions and knowledge. You will find information on every actor, director or film and of every genre in town.*

**Ain't It Cool News**                 www.aint-it-cool-news.com
Compiled from special reports by Hollywood insiders, this site covers all the inside gen: scripts, casting, pre-production, production, post-production, test screenings, marketing and so on. Run by movie obsessive Harry Knowles, the site's piercing insights and up-to-the-minute gossip has the major studios living in fear.

**All Movie Guide**                 www.allmovie.com
One of the world's largest entertainment databases, this site offers expert reviews, biographies, ratings, images, credits, and more. The glossary is a tremendously detailed reference source for a wide variety of cinema terms written by experts in the field.

**British Board of Film Classification**                 www.bbfc.co.uk
The people who decide what can and can't be shown on UK cinema screens explain what the BBFC is and does. If you want to find out why *The Unforgiven* got an 18 certificate, or the reasons *Happiness* didn't, there's a list of recent decisions.

**Cannes Film Festival**  www.festival-cannes.org

Relive more than 50 years of cinema's most prestigious competition by accessing the database of 22,000 people profiles, 5,000 films and 800 honours given out since the creation of the festival.

**Cinemachine, The Movie Review**  www.cinemachine.com
**Search Engine**

Huge index of movie reviews from a broad variety of sources, all linked to the IMdB (see below). This site provides listings of movie reviews for films of all genres, including new releases, classic films, Hollywood blockbusters, and independent features.

**Cinemas in the UK**  www.aber.ac.uk/~jwp/cinemas

Sparse but functional directory which gives the name and address of cinemas in the UK by town, together with the number of auditoria and the seating capacities where known. The webmaster certainly seems to have done his homework.

**Drew's Script-O-Rama**  www.script-o-rama.com

Vast index of movie and television scripts available on the Internet. Includes links to scripts and transcripts of movies and television shows, as well as scripts that never made it into production.

**Film.com**  www.film.com

Impressive collection of film and video criticism, with supporting material to flesh out the intrigues of the industry and keep visitors informed of film festivals. The site also previews soon-to-be-released features, hosts discussions on current issues, and offers streaming clips of movie trailers.

**FilmFestivals.com**  www.filmfestivals.com

This brilliant site has well over 7,000 pages aimed at both movie buffs and professionals, focusing on film festivals and motion picture events. It includes an excellent worldwide festival directory, a monthly bulletin board, film reviews and pertinent articles.

**The Greatest Films**                                    **www.filmsite.org**
Contains descriptive reviews and historical background, a wealth of useful film reference material (including a complete Academy Awards history), and hundreds of colourful, vintage film posters for some of the best Hollywood films of the last century.

**The Internet Movie Database**                           **www.imdb.com**
What began as the pet project of one man, Welshman Col Needham, is now one of the web's biggest and most popular sites. The tremendous catalogue covers every possible detail of more than 200,000 movie titles, 400,000 actors and nearly 40,000 directors. This is an indispensable tool, not just for film buffs but also for producers and directors checking out the CVs of their prospective cast and crew.

**Movie Bloopers**                                        **www.moviebloopers.com**
Yes, a stormtrooper really does walk into a door in *Star Wars*. An entertaining destination for film buffs who love to know everything about a film, especially when it goes wrong, this site points out the silly things that editors and directors miss in some of the biggest films ever.

**Movie Review Query Engine**                             **www.mrqe.com**
Online directory of movie reviews with more than 140,000 reviews covering 19,000 separate titles. You can browse upcoming or recent releases and search through the most popular reviews.

**Oscars History**          **www.oscars.com/history/his_index.html**
Get your Academy Award-related questions answered by an official source: the Academy historian. Search for any Academy Award nominee and get their Oscar history or use the best picture poster section to remember all 71 previous winners of the top award.

**Scoot Cinema Guide**                                    **http://cinema.scoot.co.uk**
Tell Scoot where you are and what you want to see. It'll tell you where to go and when it's on. Simple, fast and very useful.

**alt.asian.movies** – Hong-Kong superstars

**alt.cult-movies** – movies with cult followings

**alt.fan.james-bond** – where wannabe 007s swap tips

**alt.movies.indian** – get the latest on Bollywood

**alt.movies.silent** – very quiet group, this one

**rec.arts.movies.current-films** – discuss the latest releases

**rec.arts.movies.reviews** – moderated movie reviews

**rec.arts.movies.tech** – the technical aspects of the movies

**rec.arts.sf.movies** – Star Wars and others dissected

**rec.music.movies** – for soundtrack buffs

## //MUSIC

*Alongside all the e-commerce sites and CD retailers (many of which provide background material and music news for free) there are countless music obsessives online, ready to share their knowledge and debate the merits of all those obscure B-sides. Try searching Deja (www.deja.com/usenet) for newsgroup information about your favourite band, performer or composer. Whoever gets your head nodding or feet tapping – Piaf, Coltrane, Dr Dre or Shostakovich – you'll find enough data to keep you busy digging.*

**AllAboutJazz**                                        **www.allaboutjazz.com**
Introduces the leading artists in various jazz genres, identifying important new releases, providing historical information, and listing live performances. This site covers all the different styles of jazz, including modern, avant-garde, big band, fusion, groove and latin.

**All Music Guide**                              www.allmusic.com
One of the world's largest entertainment databases for music, the totally excellent All Music Guide offers reviews, biographies, ratings, images, and credits in thousands of descriptive categories, including jazz, rap, rock and folk.

**Classical Music on the Web**           www.musicweb.uk.net
Focusing on British composers, this is packed with reviews of both classic and contemporary scores, complemented by in-depth explanatory articles to make it a must for serious fans.

**Classical Net**                              www.classical.net
Explains how you can find classical music on the Internet, providing a road map to identify music that might be of interest. The site is organised by musical periods that correspond roughly to overall historical stylistic trends in music. The CD Buying Guide includes thousands of suggestions.

**Encyclopedia of the Blues**          www.blueflamecafe.com
A biographical encyclopedia of the great blues singers, including Charley Patton and Stevie Ray Vaughan. There are also links to Blues sites around the world.

**HymnSite.com**                              www.hymnsite.com
If you like to belt out a psalm or are a member of a church choir, you'll want to take a look at this site, which has thousands of hymns posted. You are encouraged to download and enjoy any of the music that you find here – it's all copyright free.

**Music History**                    www.ipl.org/exhibit/mushist
Very brief overview of major periods with representative samples in RealAudio. The site is organised according to the eras of history, beginning with the Middle Ages and stopping off in the Renaissance and Romantic period.

**Music365**                                  www.music365.com
One of the best British music offerings on the net, this vast and opinionated site is a great place to research additions to your CD

collection, mixing music news and reviews with a comprehensive gig guide. The archive search is ponderous, but there is no doubting the value of the material here.

**Rough Guide to Rock**              **www.roughguide.com/rock**
Biographies of nearly 1,400 bands and artists collated from the opinions of hundreds of contributors. Every aspect of rock is covered, as are the worlds of dance, pop, and soul. Entries also feature reviews of the most worthwhile CDs.

**Songfile**              **http://songfile.snap.com/index_2.html**
A comprehensive guide to sheet music, this site lets you search through more than 62,000 lyrics. The instruments and books page allows you to look for music-related books and explore some excellent musical instrument links.

---

## Newsgroups

**alt.gothic** – get dark

**alt.music.acid-jazz** – stay funky

**alt.music.dance** – stay up all night

**alt.music.independent** – stay at home

**alt.music.lyrics** – sing in the shower

**alt.music.world** – global rhythms

**alt.rock-n-roll** – rock around the clock

**rec.music.classical** – brush up your Beethoven

**rec.music.country.western** – saddle up here

**rec.music.folk** – dig out those sandals

**rec.music.reviews** – dissect the latest releases

## //MP3 SITES

*MP3 – the controversial file format that lets you download any song you want, in high-quality stereo, straight to your hard drive – has taken the music industry by storm. Bear in mind that to be able to play an MP3 on your PC you have to download and install special software, such as can be found at **www.sonique.com**. Or you can buy a Walkman-like MP3 player and take your music with you. Do this before you start downloading files, otherwise you're going to get pretty frustrated.*

**Lycos Music MP3 Search**                    **http://mp3.lycos.com**
With over a million of the freshest MP3s, Lycos' search engine is the world's largest MP3 site. Just type in the name of your favourite band or song title and marvel as the site returns countless listening options.

**MP3.com**                                   **www.mp3.com**
This is the premier MP3 provider, allowing you to discover, listen to and store and organise your music collection.

**MP3 guide from About.com**        **http://mp3.about.com**
One of the best destinations for MP3 news, this site explains how to find loads of free files – courtesy of those ever-reliable folks at About.com. Learn how to find, play and create music files for your personal computer.

**MP3now.com**                                **www.mp3now.com**
Hugely detailed users guide covering all the MP3 angles. There is an excellent beginners' guide for anyone finding their feet, with tips on finding MP3s (including the Top 30 search engines) and reviews of MP3 software and hardware.

**Napster**                                   **www.napster.com**
Shaking up the music industry, Napster is a revolutionary way of thinking about music online. Once installed, the application searches the Internet for your requested track and downloads it directly from any connected computer. Crucially, this is free.

**Newsgroups**

**alt.binaries.mp3.bootlegs** – where to get those less than legal MP3s

**alt.music.mp3** – all the latest MP3 news

**alt.music.mp3.napster** – the revolution is here

## //NEWS & NEWSPAPERS

*The big news providers of the old media – newspapers, magazines and TV – have all invested heavily in an online presence, and regularly updated news is available on demand and tailored to your individual requirements. Unconstrained by the space and time considerations that limit newspapers and television, the web makes it easy to find out extensive background on even the most distant and obscure stories. If you're looking for a particular newspaper online, http://newspapers.start4all.com will give you the right URL.*

**Amnesty**                                        **www.amnesty.org**
The single best source of information on human rights violations around the world. You can find a complete archive of news releases dating back to 1995 in the library, which also has an A-Z listing of Amnesty's country reports.

**Ananova**                                       **www.ananova.com**
An ambitious attempt by the UK's Press Association to personalise their news delivery service, Ananova is a virtual newscaster designed to appeal to the masses. If you've got a fast connection you'll be able to enjoy the latest news read live – otherwise this attractive young lady is more hassle than she's worth.

**BBC News**                                  **http://news.bbc.co.uk**
The BBC has invested in the Internet in a big way, and it seems to be paying off. Not only is news updated as it happens, but the site's

excellent search engine makes it easy to trawl back through the archives if you are researching a particular news story.

**CNN**                                    **www.cnn.com**
One of the longest-established and slickest Internet news sites from one of America's foremost news providers. As well as reading the latest stories you can access archives covering international politics, technology and space news. The in-depth reports are supplemented by video and audio extras.

**Greenpeace UK**                 **www.greenpeace.org.uk**
Details of all the latest campaigns, and background on long running issues such as the head-to-head with Monsanto, efforts to save the nuclear test ban treaty and attempts to stop the UK government licensing oil exploration around the historic World Heritage site of St Kilda.

**Inside China**                    **www.insidechina.com**
In addition to daily news, the site offers concise news reviews plus political and historical material on China. The homepage hosts a population tracker – showing that numbers of Chinese have doubled since 1950.

**The Irish Times**                    **www.ireland.com**
Ireland's leading quality national daily newspaper. Its online offering has all the news you would expect, but also acts as a comprehensive portal into everything Irish. Whether you are researching a holiday or business opportunity, start here.

**ITN**                                    **www.itn.co.uk**
A well organised service, but it fails to link current stories with previous ones. From a researcher's point of view, it's a frustrating case of click and hope. You enter your query into the site's search engine and browse through the results it produces, and there's no easy way of looking at a big issue in any detail.

**The Korean Central News Agency**        **www.kcna.co.jp**
The only agency in North Korea. News is transmitted in English,

Russian and Spanish. The KCNA ensures uniform delivery of news and other information to the country's mass media, but its brutalist design makes this a destination for hardcore Stalinists only.

## McSpotlight.org www.mcspotlight.org

Created during the controversial McLibel trial, this site is still expanding, providing a global network for protestors as they attempt to circumvent McDonald's attempts to silence them. Extensive information on McDonald's approach to the environment, free speech and censorship make this the place to get the beef on the beef.

## Moreover.com www.moreover.com

Whizzy software enables this brainy site to pick news from more than 1,500 editorial sources, providing 'webfeeds' of headline links in more than 200 categories. This makes the site a good place to track down hard-to-find information, and the Moreover database search works on concepts as well as keywords.

## Mother Jones www.motherjones.com

Named after a pioneer labour organiser, this site is a good place to research issues such as globalisation. The articles challenge conventional wisdom, expose abuses of power and attempt to offer fresh alternatives.

## Muslim News www.muslimnews.co.uk

Provides objective news and views for Muslims in the UK. This site has exposed what it sees as the media's anti-Muslim stance and Islamophobia on various issues – political, education, employment and religion.

## NewsDirectory www.newsdirectory.com

Guide to English-language news and media online, with well-organised links to more than 7,600 newspaper and magazine websites worldwide. Also includes a comprehensive series of links to Internet broadcasts and archive resources.

### News Index           www.newsindex.com

This is a comprehensive, up-to-the-minute news-only search engine. Enter a keyword and it returns stories from wherever the word is found online.

### NewsNow           www.newsnow.co.uk

Updated every five minutes, this British rival to Newshub (www.newshub.com) is superior in every way. It provides some of the freshest news on the web – click on a headline that takes your fancy and you'll go straight to that story. You can also search the last month's headlines.

### NewsTrawler           www.newstrawler.com

A search engine for news on the Internet, with immense potential as a research tool. From the homepage it's easy to search articles from the archives of hundreds of online news, magazine and journal sources around the world. Some will, however, charge you to look.

### New York Times           www.nytimes.com

Full access to up-to-the minute coverage from one of the USA's leading newspapers. There's an archive of *New York Times* articles going back to 1996. You can view summaries free of charge; the full text costs $2.50 per article.

### News Unlimited           www.newsunlimited.co.uk

Excellent offering from the UK's *Guardian* newspaper that includes original editorial content updated daily, 24-hour breaking news, interactive features and bulletin boards, and in-depth special reports including hundreds of links, original material, documents and statistics.

### Oneworld.net           www.oneworld.org

This site aims to bear witness to the unnecessary suffering in the world, but it's also a vastly informative gateway to development issues on the web. Guides explain key global issues such as migration, and there are sections for academics and experts.

**Out There News**                                    www.megastories.com

Provides detailed investigations of the topics in the news in an original, interactive fashion. Each topic is presented in a refreshingly balanced way, with a real attempt to put the latest developments in detailed historical context. The site covers subjects as diverse as China's relationship with Taiwan and the (rapidly fading) impact of Princess Diana's death.

**The Paperboy**                                      www.thepaperboy.com

With links to over 4,000 newspapers you'd expect this site to be backed by a major international news organisation. It's a surprise then to find that it's a one-man show based in Western Australia. A brilliant demonstration of how the Internet allows Joe Schmoe to compete with the big boys.

**ResearchBuzz!**                                     www.researchbuzz.com

Covers the latest developments in the world of Internet research, with updates on search engines, browser technology, online collections of information and web directories. If in doubt, the final question is, 'would a reference librarian find it useful?' If the answer is yes, in it goes.

**Reuters**                                           www.reuters.com

The world's leading provider of financial information and news helps you delve deeper into the headlines, kicking off with a running stock ticker on the homepage. The advanced search lets you search for documents by language.

**Russia Today**                                      www.russiatoday.com

A vast site for a vast country, this is a Westerner's best source of news coverage for Russia and the CIS. Find out about the Federal Assembly, Federation Council, State Duma, and the Executive Branch and get biographies of the important politicians. The entire constitution is also online.

## Newsgroups

**alt.current-events.kashmir** – potential nuclear flashpoint

**alt.news.media** – don't believe the hype

**alt.journalism.newpapers** – fringe (as opposed to gutter) journalism

**uk.media-newspapers** – Fleet Street on the ropes

**uk.net.news.announce** – all the latest Internet news

## //PARENTING

From family planning to pacifying angry teens, the Internet has information for all new and prospective parents. If you're about to give birth, you'll find the net an endless source of reassurance and encouragement. You can talk to other mums and mums-to-be and tap into a global knowledge base. Parents of older children will find oodles of general advice.

**Babynamer.com**                    **www.babynamer.com**
Service dedicated to helping new parents choose the perfect name for their child, with a database containing 20,000 names. You can move easily from familiar favourites to nicknames, explore different spellings and non-English equivalents. You will also find a huge number of unfamiliar names.

**Babyworld**                    **www.babyworld.co.uk**
A vibrant community where new and expectant parents can share experiences and support, and a popular destination for women keen to learn about the their bodies, their babies, and childbirth.

**KidsDoctor**                    **www.kidsdoctor.com**
Since 1996 the KidsDoctor has answered thousands of questions about child health. The site lists some of the most typical and useful, but if you don't find your problem dealt with here, you can email your own question.

**Netparenting.com** www.netparenting.com
All the information you need to know about Internet safety for children, software filtering and more. There are also hundreds of online entertainment and education ideas for children.

**Okparenting** www.okparenting.co.uk
Based on the idea that collaboration and co-operation are the best ways to approach parenthood, this site lets users search for information and share their worries, passions and concerns with others. The helpful working parent's section discusses maternity leave, babysitting and the pros and cons of different childcare options.

**ParentsPlace.com** www.parentsplace.com
America's first online parenting community, this site is run by two stay-at-home parents who believe other parents are the best source of information on parenting. Whether you are interested in fertility, pregnancy, breastfeeding, or your child's development or health, the site's extensive archive of feature articles should help.

**Savlon First Aid** www.familyfirstaid.co.uk
Ok, so it's primarily a plug for Savlon's first aid products – but this site is a useful introduction to basic life-saving skills and has tips for eliminating dangers in the home. The holiday first aid section has a list of medical phrases in several languages. It is sometimes difficult to read the instructions, so don't come here in an emergency!

**Surfing the Net with Children** www.surfnetkids.com
Fabulous archive of website reviews on subjects such as butterflies, Houdini, online encyclopedias, crossword puzzles and the Wright brothers. The site is edited by nationally syndicated American newspaper columnist, Barbara J. Feldman.

**UK Parents** www.ukparents.co.uk
Set up to compete with the successful US parenting sites, this British site has information tailored to your needs or your child's age – so there are sections for toddlers, pre-schoolers and Dads.

There's advice on breast and bottle-feeding and a very handy A-Z of child health.

**Urbia**                                                      www.urbia.co.uk

You are not alone with your family problems. Advice and information on everything from health and pregnancy to sex and shopping – as well as providing a place for you to share your concerns with other parents.

---

**Newsgroups**

**alt.parents** – pool that knowledge

**alt.parents-teens** – how to cope with adolescence

**altsupport.single-parents** – support group for single parents

**alt.support** – a shoulder to cry on when it all gets too much

**uk.people.parents** – parents swap tips

## //PEOPLE FINDERS

*Frustrating, but there is no definitive way to search for someone online. Email addresses are issued by a huge variety of companies and Internet providers, so there no online equivalent to the telephone directory. This is unlikely to change in the foreseeable future.*

**Bigfoot**                                                    www.bigfoot.com

The biggest email directory on the Internet, with the most accurate white pages anywhere. Combine that with fast and easy searching and this is an excellent place to start looking, particularly if you are trying to find someone in the US.

**Cameo**                                              http://cameo.bvdep.com

Cameo is an Internet service that provides information on the 46 million adults registered on the UK Electoral Roll. It's quick and easy to use, but it is designed for business use. Packages start at a steep £3,100.

**Electoral Roll Information for the UK**     www.electoralroll.com

Probably the best way to find people anywhere in UK, whether old friends or family members. They charge £15 if they find who you're looking for, and are paid on a 'no success – no fee' basis – no advance payment is required. A cheaper option than splashing out on Cameo.

**Find A Grave**                          www.findagrave.com

A gigantic virtual graveyard, this site has been locating the final resting places of the famous since 1995. They recently began listing the graves of ordinary folk too, starting off with 2.5 million burial records. Browsing these pages is a great way to research colourful personalities and (for the morbid minded) to locate interesting graves to visit.

**International Directories**        www.worldpages.com/global

To search Business and People Search directories around the world, select a country from the pull-down menu and click on Search. Includes 117 million US and Canadian White and Yellow Pages listings, nine million email addresses and links to more than 350 online international directories.

**The Internet Address Finder**                    www.iaf.net

The choice of millions of US Internet users for searching and finding the names, email addresses, and increasingly video phone contacts of Internet users. Contains more than 6.5 million names.

**UK Private Investigators**     www.ukprivateinvestigators.com

Investigation company offering discreet and professional surveillance, tracing missing persons, friends and family, debtors and probably lots of people who would rather not be found.

**Yahoo! People Finder**              www.yahoo.com/search/people

Search and be found in one of the Internet's biggest email directories. You can search for email addresses by name only, or you can include any portion of a user's domain to narrow your search. While you're looking, register yourself in the Yahoo! People Search email directory so others can find you.

**WhoWhere**                                    **www.whowhere.com**
WhoWhere is one of the best online people finders, mainly because it was the earliest, and has consequently had more time to built up a database of names.

## //PERSONAL FINANCE

*Keen to squirrel some money away for a rainy day? The Internet makes it easy to get solid advice on making your money work for you. This is a brief selection; you'll find much more on this subject in the* **Virgin Internet Money Guide**.

**The Council of Mortgage Lenders**              **www.cml.org.uk**
The trade association for mortgage lenders in the UK, whose members undertake around 98 per cent of UK residential mortgage lending. This site provides a forum for anyone wishing to discuss their mortgage with the professionals before they commit.

**FT Your Money**                              **www.ftyourmoney.com**
This is a brilliant UK service designed to help you manage and maximise your money. The site is independent and authoritative, and concentrates on personal finance issues that are relevant to everyone.

**Moneynet**                                    **www.moneynet.co.uk**
The first British site to publish a comprehensive and independent overview of the products available in the personal finance sector. It includes details of mortgage and savings products from over 100 providers.

**MoneyWorld UK**                              **www.moneyworld.co.uk**
A useful analysis of the main players in the Internet banking marketplace that compares the offerings currently available. There's a selection of handy interactive tools designed to help you calculate your mortgage, tax, health care, insurance costs and analyse past performance for some 50 major world currencies.

**This Is Money**     www.thisismoney.com

Very practical site with informative sections covering savings and investing, mortgages, pensions, insurance and taxes. Each section has a selection of handy tools, so the saving area lists the top savings rates, recommended unit trusts and has a useful ISA centre among many other options.

## //PETS

*There's a lot of info about domesticated beasts here, whether it's a www.bigchihuahua.com or a chinchilla. Stick the name of the species or breed into a search engine and get clicking.*

**Bringing Pets to Britain**   www.maff.gov.uk/animalh/quarantine

Under the Pet Travel Scheme, or PETS for short, you may be allowed to bring pooch or puss to Britain without having to put it in quarantine. These pages explain the system and tell you about quarantine for animals that don't qualify.

**Pets.com**     www.pets.com

With expert advice from a staff of pet-industry experts and veterinarians, US-based Pets.com gives pet owners confidence that they are providing their pets with the best possible care. Lots of solid advice. If your furry, feathered or scaly friend has a problem you want explained and rectified, you can email one of the vets here and they'll do their best to help.

**Pets at Home**     www.petsathome.com

This site has a range of care guides that provide outline how to feed and house pets properly and how to keep them healthy.

**RSPCA**     www.rspca.org.uk

News, campaigns, animal advice and details of the RSPCA's history and present-day work. You can use the site to find your nearest RSPCA branch, animal centre, and clinic or animal hospital.

## Newsgroups

**alt.aquaria** – everything from goldfish to dolphins

**alt.pets** – discuss your furry, scaly or feathered friend

**rec.birds** – I really fancy your bird

**rec.pets** – more pet chat

**rec.pets.cats** – Tigger happy

**rec.pets.dogs.misc** – different ways to care for dogs

## //PICTURES

*Most of the major search engines have picture or image search facilities. Pics are often described as clip art, which basically means any electronic illustration that can be inserted into a document. At present, grabbing pictures off the Internet is something of a grey area. Technically there's nothing to stop you going to a site, right-clicking on an image you like and saving it to your hard drive, but this could be illegal.*

**ArtToday**                                          www.arttoday.com
Home to more than one million images, this is the largest searchable, categorised set of clip art, web graphics, photographs and fonts available on the Internet. All images are royalty-free.

**Barry's Clip Art Server**                    www.barrysclip art.com
There are thousands of images here, all free for you to download. You're supposed to read the disclaimer page before you start grabbing them.

**The Clip Art Connection**              www.clipartconnection.com
An award-winning place to download all types of clip art and digital imagery. If you can't find what you want on site, follow one of the hundreds of links to other places that might have it.

**Corbis**                                    **www.corbis.com**

Holds 65 million of the world's most memorable images, with more than 2.1 million available online. The site is organised into two divisions: Corbis Images, the licensing division for the creative professional, and Corbis.com, for online consumers. In both sections there is usually a fee involved.

**Ditto.com**                                  **www.ditto.com**

Provides a way of searching the web for pictures instead of text. Users are directed to the originating site on which the picture is located. If you want to reuse any picture, photo or artwork, you should obtain the permission from the copyright holder.

---

**Newsgroups**

---

**alt.binaries.picture.astro** – very black pictures

**alt.binaries.pictures.clip.art** – thousands of pics

**alt.binaries.pictures.fine-art.photos** – photographic art

**alt.pictures.pictures.wallpaper** – brighten up your desktop

**alt.binaries.ufo.files** – pictures of ufos

## //POPULATION STATISTICS

*The Internet is proving a boon for statisticians and anyone curious about the world around them. You can keep track of population growth, and cross-reference data to draw out demographic trends. For school geography projects or economic research, there's a wide range of useful sites.*

**Global Statistics**                           **www.xist.org**

A nicely designed site that lets you find out the largest, smallest and fastest growing populations around the world. You can examine population change over different time periods and do regional or continental comparisons.

**PopNet**                                   **www.popnet.org**

The most comprehensive directory of population-related sites available – searchable by topic or keyword, organisation or via a world map. Get the lowdown on demographic statistics, economics, education, environment, gender, policy and reproductive health.

**Population Reference Bureau**                   **www.prb.org**

Hugely informative site that monitors population trends and looks at the demographics of family planning, ageing, crime, immigration, changing family structure, minorities' status, and environmental degradation. Sobering stuff.

**UN Population Information Network**      **www.undp.org/popin**

Typically vast destination from the UN that lets researchers access data from one of the world's most authoritative information gatherers. The site is text-heavy, but worth persevering with, because the depth of information here is unrivalled.

**Your Nation**                            **www.your-nation.com**

This fast-loading, refreshingly simple site will prove invaluable for anyone who has ever searched fruitlessly for a way to compare different countries. The possibilities are almost endless: rank countries by a yardstick of your choice, display country summaries and compare statistics from literacy to GDP.

## //QUOTATIONS

*'To be or not to be?' Is that the question? As well as all the classic quotes, the web brings you quote archives on some of the most peculiar topics imaginable. Out of the mouths of babes ...*

**Book of Famous Quotes**            **www.geocities.com/haythum**

Lots of sections and categories and hilarious cheesy background muzak makes searching this site rewarding and fun. Includes a recently added Famous Quotations search engine. Browse by category, author or alphabetically.

## A Dictionary of Scientific Quotations

http://naturalscience.com/dsqhome.html

From Archimedes ('Give me a place to stand, and I will move the Earth') to Richard Woolley, the British Astronomer Royal who said 'Space travel is utter bilge' in 1956 – a year before *Sputnik*, this is a revealing list of famous science-related quotations.

## Engineering Quotes

www.fen.bris.ac.uk/civil/resource/engquot1.htm

'A common mistake that people make when trying to design something completely foolproof is to underestimate the ingenuity of complete fools.' So says Douglas Adams in this excellent collection of civil engineering and engineering-related quotes which contains a nice mix of idealistic, cynical and humorous entries.

## Famous Quotations Network

www.famous-quotations.com

An accessible network of sites that tell you what people said. Famous sayings here are sorted by categories and subjects, making this a usable destination for any student, researcher, or lover of pithy phrases.

## IMdB Movie Quotes Browser

http://us.imdb.com/Sections/Quotes

Hasta la vista, baby. The staff at the Internet Movie Database don't spend all their days scouring movie scripts and transcribing them, but they are happy to let users submit their favourite quotes to add to this list. They don't have every great line from every movie, but this is pretty comprehensive.

## Mathematical Quotation Server

http://math.furman.edu/~mwoodard/mqs/mquot.shtml

Although you might disagree with Siméon Poisson's claim that 'life is good for only two things, discovering mathematics and teaching mathematics,' this site has a fascinating range of quotes relating to a subject that has been called the purest art.

**QuoteArchive.com**  www.quotearchive.com
Incredibly sparse design gets you wondering about the content,
but you will discover that this is a conscious decision that makes
finding the quote you are looking for hassle free. The A-Z listing
covers everyone from Alexander the Great to Frank Zappa.

**Quoteland.com**  www.quoteland.com
The best place to find offbeat sayings. The site's purpose is not to
repeat the classics but to get useful, relevant quotes that have yet
to pass into history.

**QuoteWorld**  www.quoteworld.org
All the memorable lines from all the memorable movies are here,
but it isn't just a movie quote site – the classics are here too.

**The Quotations Archive**  www.aphids.com/quotes
Browse quotations by subject, alphabetically by author, or use the
search engine to generate a listing of quotations containing
selected keywords. So many options, so little time.

## //RELIGION

*Although we are yet to witness the first Internet church, there's no
doubt that the Net's emergence, coinciding with the millennial
celebrations, has initiated an explosion of interest in religion of all
faiths. Theologians and believers searching for inspiration will like
these sites, but agnostics and atheists should probably steer clear.*

**Adherents**  www.adherents.com
All about those who believe or belong. Membership and
congregation statistics for over 4,200 religions, churches,
denominations, religious bodies, faith groups, tribes, cultures and
movements.

**Church of England**  www.cofe.anglican.org
This site has both a spiritual and a physical dimension. First and
foremost it is about proclaiming the name of Jesus Christ. You can

also search the site for details of services and locations for every Anglican church in the UK.

**Facets of Religion**  www.bcca.org/~cvoogt/Religion
Brilliant site with hundreds of links to the great faiths: Buddhism, Christianity, Confucianism, Hinduism, Islam, Jainism, Judaism, Sikhism, Taoism and Zoroastrianism are all extensively featured. You can also find ancient religions, cults and magical religions.

**HinduNet**  www.hindunet.org
Monumental explanatory site with images, directories and event calendars on Hinduism. Sections cover Hindu scriptures, festivals and history and take a close look at Gods, Sages and Gurus. There's also a section on yoga.

**Religion-Online**  www.religion-online.org
Designed to assist professors, scholars and seekers interested in exploring religious issues, this site hosts texts by religious scholars. More than 1,500 articles cover such topics as the Old and New Testament, theology, ethics, comparative religion, pastoral care, counselling, worship, missions and religious education.

**Religious and Sacred Texts**  www.davidwiley.com/religion.html
Scriptures of all faiths are presented here in the hope that you will use them to find the Truth. Browse everything from the *Bhagavad Gita* to the *Tibetan Book of the Dead* via the Dead Sea Scrolls and sacred Confucian Texts.

**Religious Tolerance**  www.religioustolerance.org
Examines some of the many thousands of non-Christian religions and ethical systems of the world. Covers new religious movements from benign groups to doomsday cults, and relays news items from around the world demonstrating the evils of religious intolerance.

## Newsgroups

**alt.atheism** – whaddayamean, you're not a believer?

**alt.hindu** – Brahma, Shiva and Vishnu in earnest conversation

**alt.religion.christian** – scripture union

**alt.religion.islam** – plan your pilgrimage to Mecca

**talk.religion.misc** – general religious chat

## //RESTAURANT FINDERS

*Finding and booking a table for dinner should work a treat on the net, ideally combining a mass of searchable information with the convenience of browsing menus and prices before you decide. Yet of the clutch of online guides, few allow you to book. You'll just have to pick up the phone.*

**Eats.co.uk**                                    **www.eats.co.uk**
This site isn't pretty, but it's fast. Scotland is especially well covered, and 462 English towns are listed. There are useful links to restaurant websites, menus and wine lists.

**Harden's Top UK Restaurants**                   **www.hardens.com**
Researched with the aid of the *Observer* newspaper, this incorporates more consumer feedback than any other national guide does. Currently the London Guide is accessible online after registration.

**The Restaurant Guide**                          **www.restaurant.org.au**
One hopes the food is a little more exciting than this brilliantly functional, but nevertheless badly presented guide to the restaurants of Australia. Sure it's easy and gets the job done, but so do fish & chips.

**Simply Food**                                   **www.simplyfood.co.uk**
Gives details of 25,000 UK restaurants, cafes and pubs serving food. These listings boast a ratings system, maps and reader comments,

plus a beautifully illustrated, informative selection of survival guides for Chinese, Japanese and Thai food.

**Toptable.co.uk**                                    **www.toptable.co.uk**
This site offers romantic venues for intimate dinners, Michelin-starred restaurants to impress clients, and reviews of hip destinations. There's a search section and a daily selection that leapfrogs waits at a raft of famous restaurants where it is usually impossible to book less than six weeks ahead.

**UK Restaurant Guide**                    **www.ukrestaurantguide.com**
An innovative guide offering links, reviews and general information about the UK's great (and not so great) restaurants. You can go directly to restaurant sites by choosing a type of cuisine, or use the search facility to locate one in your area of choice.

**Zagat.com**                                         **www.zagat.com**
This quick-loading destination delivers accurate reviews for more than 20,000 restaurants, all based on your opinions. Pick a city to get started – these are mostly American, although Zagat has just began international expansion.

---

**Newsgroups**

---

**alt.restaurants** – general foodie chat

**alt.restaurants.professionals** – where chefs compare notes

**nyc.food** – eating out in Manhattan

**rec.food.restaurants** – dining out in general

**uk.food+drink.restaurants** – independent guide to UK restaurants

## //SCIENCE

*Surfing the web for useful information is comparable to sifting for gold in an ore-rich field. It's rewarding but arduous: on the Internet you can struggle through endless streams of badly*

*researched features before chancing on enlightenment. Here's a selection of the web's best science sites.*

**Amusement Park Physics**                     www.learner.org/ exhibits/parkphysics

If you've ever braved a big roller-coaster, you'll have admired the mechanics and pondered the dangers. By helping you build your own virtual ride, this informative site demonstrates how the laws of physics can be used to simulate danger and make sure you're actually safe.

**Bad Astronomy**                     www.badastronomy.com

Frustrated by the pseudoscientific misinformation spread about astronomy, this site sets out to put things right. It takes the misconceptions of TV sci-fi as a starting point to explain the true science.

**Circlemakers.org**                     www.circlemakers.org

Takes an intriguing look at Britain's crop circle enigma, making it the ideal place for anyone interested in these notorious additions to the countryside. A stunning collection of formations illustrates the evolution of the technique.

**Dr Matrix's Web World of Science**                     www.scientium.com/ drmatrix

Dr Matrix searches for sites that serve an active scientific purpose and the result is one of the best scientific resources on the web. The home page offers topics as diverse as anthropology and SETI (the search for other life in the universe) – and each section is full of useful advice, news and links.

**Kid's Science from About.com**          http://kidscience.about.com

Who was Albert Einstein? What amazing discoveries did he make? This site presents serious science in a fun, accessible way for kids of all ages.

**NASA**                     www.nasa.gov

A vast resource covering every aspect of space exploration and related scientific research imaginable. Includes fact sheets on NASA and its programs; a daily newsletter with articles and press releases on recent activities; and sections on research in aeronautics, human space flight, space science, and earth science.

### Nature.com     www.nature.com

One of the world's most authoritative science magazines publishes cutting-edge research online. You can search the archive for detailed background information going back to January 1997. If you need more, a magazine subscription gives you access to a collection of specialised databases.

### New Scientist     www.newscientist.com

This tremendously helpful site offers a huge range of content, much of it unique. One of the most useful sections is the database of everyday science questions, which answers questions like 'why is the sky blue?' and 'why don't penguins' feet freeze?'

### Volcano World     http://volcano.und.nodak.edu

Introduces you to real volcanologists and explains how to become one, and also has a mass of information on one of nature's most violent phenomena. The site has an excellent range of case studies from volcanoes around the world.

### The Why Files     http:// whyfiles.news.wisc.edu

How often do news articles leave you wondering about the scientific details they discuss? This excellent site explains the science behind the headlines, with topics like killer tsunamis and chemical weapons explained with the aid of easily comprehensible diagrams. Informative and enjoyable.

---

### Newsgroups

---

**sci.biology** – dissecting frogs and all that

**sci.math** – mathematical discussions and pursuits

**sci.physics** – Galileo and chums get serious

**sci.skeptic** – sceptics discussing pseudo-science

**sci.space.misc** – is there life on Mars?

## //SPORT

*The source of more pub arguments than almost anything else. Yet how often is there a copy of Wisden to hand when you need to prove that the batsman was Holding while the bowler was Willey? Now these debates can be settled once and for all.*

**The Climbing**                     **www.fm.bs.dlr.de/misc/**
**Dictionary**                       **climbing/climbing_dict.html**
Rock climbing is a dangerous sport which requires careful decision making and information you can trust. Helpfully, this site has definitions of American and English climbing terms.

**Cricketbase**                      **www.cricketbase.com**
The most comprehensive online database of One Day International and Test cricket, with a huge array of statistics, including: results for every Test ever played, complete stats for every player and all One Day International results.

**Golfcourses.org**                  **www.golfcourses.org**
Well-designed destination built to help golf lovers choose from Britain's 1,600 clubs, making it easy to find out about the facilities and green fees of each potential course. The site is searchable by country, town or club.

**The International Rugby Board**        **www.irfb.com**
The IRB is the world governing and law-making body for the Game of Rugby Union. This site has all the laws of the game, comprehensive fixture lists and an easily searchable results archive.

**Olympics**                         **www.olympics.com/eng**
It's all here: highlights, records, histories and explanatory guides for every sport in the Games. This site has the most comprehensive online guide for every event, including news, features, history,

rules, records and step-by-step technical details on all 28 sports in the Games.

**Scrum.com**                                    **www.scrum.com**

This excellent offering has extensive news, tables and squad and club information for rugby fans around the world. There is a global archive of who's who in rugby, a handy primer for anyone new to the game and decent coverage of the women's game.

**Soccerbase**                                  **www.soccerbase.com**

Vast, up-to-date source of British football data on the Internet. Contains a huge array of statistics, including results for every single league and cup games ever played by all English and Scottish League clubs, including European competitions.

**SwimNet**                                    **www.swimnet.co.uk**

If you're keen to take up swimming as a sport, but have no idea where to start, go to this well organised site, which has links to scores of swimming clubs around the UK. There's also lots of news from swimming events around the world.

**The Where to Fish Directory**         **www.where-to-fish.com**

Claims to be Earth's largest online fishing information service, with more than 3,000 pages covering fishing locations around the world. Simply type in the name of the river or still water you want to fish, and the site delivers contacts and cost details.

**Wisden**                                      **www.wisden.co.uk**

Authoritative Test records updated every week, as well as The Wisden verdict on England's performance in every day's play in Tests and one-day internationals. It's a grim job, but someone has to do it.

---

**Newsgroups**

---

**alt.fish** – it was this big ...

**rec.running** – chariots of fire

**rec.autos.sport.f1** – Formula 1 motor racing

**rec.sport.baseball** – pitch it up here

**rec.sport.cric.info** – statistical heaven

**rec.sport.golf** – enthusiasts swap club tales

**rec.sport.rugby.union** – everything for the player or supporter

**rec.sport.soccer** – the world's greatest game

**rec.sport.tennis** – anyone for tennis?

**uk.sport.football** – the one-horse race. And the two-horse race

## //TRANSPORT

*Plan your route here, with detailed maps and route planners that organise your journey for you. You can check for roadworks and get the latest weather news – and even find the details of the locations of speed cameras.*

**Airport and Air Travel Guide**          **www.airwise.com**
Includes an independent guide to airports and their facilities around the world. All the latest on airline alliances, smoking policies, aircraft safety and air-conditioning systems. Enter the airline, flight number and arrival date to get worldwide arrival times for major airlines.

**Aviation Safety Network**          **http://aviation-safety.net**
Grimly fascinating site provides up-to-date, authoritative information on airliner accidents and safety issues. The Accident Database lists all events that have resulted in a plane being damaged beyond repair, including bad weather and acts of aggression.

**European rail timetables  http://mercurio.iet.unipi/it/home.html**
Masses of stuff about trains in Europe, for railway fans as well as for travellers who want to travel Europe by train. Plenty of links to

the sites of the European national railways, online timetables and travel planners – and some insanely detailed trainspotter pages.

### London Transport      www.londontransport.co.uk
Within this site you will find general information on London's hopelessly overburdened and undermanned bus and tube services, including maps, fares, times of first and last trains and a guide to bus routes.

### RAC Route Planner      www.rac.co.uk/services
Whether you're popping around the corner or driving across the Continent, you'll find the fastest route for your journey here.

### The Speedtrap Bible      www.speed-trap.co.uk
Believe it or not, local councils in the UK publish their own speed camera location sites in the public domain. These pages spill the beans, so you know where they are. The road with the most cameras? The A40 between Cheltenham and Oxford, with a staggering 19 along a 40-mile stretch.

### Subway Navigator      www.subwaynavigator.com
An online program that helps you plot your journey on public transport in over sixty cities around the world. You get a detailed description of your journey and the best route to take, the estimated time of arrival and a map of the route.

### Tubehell.com      www.tubehell.com
All Londoners are united by transport woes, and the ancient, cramped underground rail network helps make life miserable for 2.5 million people every day. This site offers reliable, up-to-the-minute travel news and a guide to places to go near each station.

### UK Railways on the Net      www.rail.co.uk
Good-looking Flash site that links to UK train operating companies, timetables and other travel services available on the Net. Go to www.railtrack.co.uk if you just want timetables.

**UK Travel**  www.ukonline.co.uk/content/travel.html

Taking a break this year? Want to know where you can get all the right information to allow your holiday to go smoothly? This travel guide will give every resource you need. Whether it's in the UK or on a remote island, you will never be more than a click away from your favourite destination.

---

**Newsgroups**

---

**aus.rail** – Australian train discussions

**misc.transport.rail.americas** – railroads in North and South America

**misc.transport.urban-transit** – public transport systems

**rec.travel.cruises** – travel in style

**uk.railway** – trainspotting, British style

**uk.rec.waterways** – get on your barge

## //WEATHER

*In the UK, weather is a national obsession, but the weather affects lives and livelihoods all over the world, every day. If you're planning an important weekend break or just want to see what it's like on the beach in San Paulo, the Internet has weather reports immediately available. Sniff the air here.*

**The BBC Weather Centre**  www.bbc.co.uk/weather

Produces around a hundred forecasts every weekday, as well as additional broadcasts over the weekend. This site includes the European Sun Index, the shipping forecast and a summary of the year so far.

**European Centre for**  www.ecmwf.int
**Medium-Range Weather Forecasts**

Even the most complex weather systems are governed by simple physical laws, and these brave meteorologists do their best to use them to predict the weather a long way into the future.

**Impact Weather**                    www.impactweather.co.uk
Leading source of detailed localised weather forecasts. If you're
planning a fête or hiring a marquee, they'll do their best to help –
for a £7.50 charge.

**Intellicast**                           www.intellicast.com
Specialised weather information to help plan outdoor and weather
sensitive activities like golfing, sailing, hiking, skiing or relaxing at
the beach. There are an unbelievable 250,000 pages of detailed
weather information here.

**The Met Office**                        www.meto.govt.uk
More than just weather forecasts. This UK governmental
organisation has a wide range of responsibilities, helping farmers,
airports and emergency services to get it right.

**OnlineWeather.com**                  www.onlineweather.com
Links to over 6,000 city forecasts around the world, and an extensive
selection of climate data for most countries, including detailed
sailing forecasts for coastal waters around the UK and N Ireland.

**The Weather Channel**                   www.weather.com
A great place to learn more about the climate, with a mix of fun
and serious material. The site features current conditions and
forecasts for over 1,700 cities world wide, along with local and
regional radar images.

**Weather from About.com**         http://weather.about.com
Want to know what the weather was like the day you were born?
Trying to find out how cold it was that day your car broke down?
Find out how, courtesy of this brilliant guide to every imaginable
aspect of the weather.

**Weather**                            www.wunderground.com/
**Underground**                            global/UK.html
As well as all the latest weather reports for UK cities, this site has
climate data for the last five years. Go to the city you are interested
in, and use the selector box to choose a date.

**World Climate**                    **www.worldclimate.com**

Contains over 85,000 records of world climate data from a range of sources. The site is designed for a general audience interested in historical weather patterns around the world.

---

**Newsgroups**

**alt.talk.weather** – general weather chat

**alt.binaries.pictures.weather** – pics of big storms

**alt.talk.weather.snow** – watch out for the white stuff

**bit.listserv.wx-chase** – tornado chasers discussion

**uk.sci.weather** – reasoned attempts to explain Britain's bizarre weather

# 5//EDUCATIONAL RESEARCH

The Internet's origins as an academic network help to make it an unparalleled source of information for university students and academics. Researchers can work on projects simultaneously – and combine their findings immediately – no matter where they are in the world. Anyone demanding the depth and detail required for a serious piece of academic research will know that the Internet is the most accessible library on Earth. It's also the greatest homework helper ever invented, and it's only right that your children should be able to turn to it, whatever subject they are researching.

New digital media have the potential to empower pupils and significantly raise educational standards. Children often find using computers more stimulating than watching their teachers explain on the blackboard or reading a dry textbook. As connection speeds improve, the net is going to have an even bigger impact on education than it is having already.

**Parental advisory**
Surfing is a family affair. To stop kids from seeing the adult-only content on the web, make sure your browser or protection software is set up to block such sites, and install your PC in a family room where you can keep an eye on what they're doing. You may also wish to subscribe to a family-friendly ISP like AOL, which will do the job for you. There's much fuller advice about safe surfing in **The Virgin Family Internet Guide**.

Meanwhile a good strategy is to bookmark a child-friendly home page from which kids can start their enquiries. Organised by librarians, Kids Click (at **http://sunsite.berkeley.edu/kidsclick!**) lists safe sites for kids. Yahoo! provides a searchable directory at **www.yahooligans.com**. It's an excellent place for children to begin their explorations. Each site is carefully checked to ensure its content and any links it contains are appropriate for kids aged 7-12. 'Sleazy, slimy, hateful, hideous, harmful, pornographic, or prejudiced' sites are rejected. Ask Jeeves for Kids (**www.ajkids.com**) is another essential bookmark.

## //ADDRESS BOOK

### Starting points

*Later on in this chapter you'll find listings of specialist sites for the most popular academic disciplines, but in this section you will find an eclectic selection of uniformly excellent wide-ranging sites. Whatever stage you or your child is at, these are the best destinations to begin your educational research.*

**BBC Online Education**                    **www.bbc.co.uk/education**
You would expect Auntie's education pages to come up with the goods, and thankfully this huge site easily exceeds expectations. With a massive amount of material designed to complement the UK National Curriculum, the schools online section includes the popular Bitesize revision help. Elsewhere, the Learning Zone has material for all ages, or you can take advantage of the in-depth guide to education websites.

**Dorling Kindersley**                    **www.dk.com**
There can be few households that do not possess at least one of this excellent publisher's distinctive illustrated books. Not only does this site make it easy to order books online, but it also brings the stunning pictures and clear text of many to your PC. The Eyewitness Encyclopedia Online is a useful homework help, where kids can find out more about everything from volcanoes and Vikings to sharks and shipwrecks.

**Educating.net**                    **www.educating.net**
Hugely comprehensive US education search engine covering everything from distance learning to university degrees, continuing

education, homework help and teacher resources. Looking for an MBA from a prestigious university like Duke, a law degree that allows you to practice in your state or some of the $55 billion offered annually in college scholarships? This site has the details.

**Education Network Australia**  www.edna.edu.au
Organised around the Australian curriculum, the largest (and most useful) part of the site is the directory of more than 9,000 links to other educational websites. These selected sites are in turn connected to over 200,000 other sites – which can also be searched from here.

**Education Planet**  www.educationplanet.com
One of the best education web guides, with lesson plans, maps, news and books on site, plus a set of excellent educational links – about 100,000 learning websites, vetted and approved by teachers. There's also a vibrant educational community, with online forums, teacher training and sites of the week.

**Education Unlimited**  www.educationunlimited.co.uk
Another classy effort from the UK *Guardian* newspaper, with 24-hour breaking education news and in-depth special reports and hundreds of links to original material, documents and statistics.

**Education World**  www.education-world.com
Brilliant all-round destination. Teachers can organise lesson plans through the site, find useful information on the benefits of technology in the classroom and ideas for lessons. Students can get help with term papers and consult an extensive range of research materials, and there's lots of advice for parents, too.

**EduWeb**  www.eduweb.co.uk
Mainly for teachers, with weekly summaries of educational news items, comprehensive links to educational institutions, guides to school league tables, OFSTED (Office for Standards in Education) reports and examination results.

**Edweek**  www.edweek.org

The online version of the US *Education Week* and *Teacher* magazines, covering local, state, and national education news and issues from pre-school through to 12th grade. There are special reports on topics ranging from technology to textbooks, and brief but thorough background essays on key education issues.

**Internet for Schools**  www.internetforschools.co.uk

This site is run by the *Daily Telegraph* – one of the UK's premier newspapers – to help teachers and students get more out of the Internet. The website guide gathers together hundreds of sites in every subject from Art to PE, and the 'Virtual School' has comprehensive lesson plans accompanied by notes that clearly explain to teachers and parents the level and aims of each session.

**Learn.co.uk**  www.learn.co.uk

Top-quality online lessons and learning materials for British kids. Everything on the site has been evaluated and approved by classroom teachers at state comprehensive schools. For parents, there are features offering information and advice on schools, as well as advice on how best to help your child learn on the web.

**Learnfree**  www.learnfree.co.uk

Progress through this website as your kids grow up – it's organised by age. The pre-school section has suggestions for learning at home, and advice on choosing a school, and it takes you all the way to university. The 'Best of the Web' section points you to essential sites for further research, and kids can download instant GCSE revision guides.

**Learning.com**  www.learning.com

Cut through the chaos of the Internet and find your age, grade and subject specific information here, all reviewed by the site's own learning professionals. Teachers can find links, articles and lesson plans covering every age group from Kindergarten upwards. Parents can get details on K-12 schools and research alternatives.

**Living Library**  http://livlib.eduweb.co.uk

A beautifully designed gateway to two million (count 'em) articles covering every subject from Roman settlements to Keynesian theory – and thousands more get added each week. It's organised by topic into four hundred collections. The 'Classroom Activities' section provides teachers with ideas, examples and a template lesson plan showing how to make effective use of the site in the classroom.

**Mailbase**  www.mailbase.co.uk

The email discussion list service for the British academic and research community. Join a Mailbase list to collaborate on projects, announce conferences, arrange meetings, or just keep in touch with colleagues in your subject area. The lists cover a vast range of topics, but if they don't have one that covers your subject, they'll help you set one up.

**NISS Information Gateway**  www.niss.ac.uk

A useful UK entry-point to higher education professionals, with circulars from the Higher Education Funding Councils, Research Council reports, library catalogues and lists of academic and research vacancies. There's also up-to-date government data on those horrible funding issues.

**Schoolsnet**  www.schoolsnet.com

This British site is gradually assuming a pivotal position at the heart of the UK National Grid for Learning. At its heart is a huge guide to every school and university in the UK – including examination results and inspection reports. There's a 20,000-title strong illustrated online library, a guide to educational sites across the web and lots of stuff for pupils and teachers, including interactive lessons, essay plans and exam questions.

**SearchEdu**  www.searchedu.com

Very focused, this unique search engine only looks at sites provided by educational institutions – most links here end in .edu, .ac.uk or the like. As well as the academic material you'd expect from universities, schools, and libraries, there's quick access to reference tools such as dictionaries, thesauri, encyclopedias, and biographies.

**Spartacus Educational**                    **www.spartacus.schoolnet.co.uk**
One of the best British educational offerings on the Net. Made up of an extensive series of encyclopedias, the site provides a huge range of content useful for both pupils and teachers. Text within entries is linked to other relevant pages, making it easy for students to click through to deeper levels for their research.

**Webmonkey**                                **http://hotwired.lycos.com/**
**for Kids**                                 **webmonkey/kids**
The grown-up Webmonkey is a comprehensive source of advice for anyone setting up a website. This brilliant sub-site shows children everything they need to know about building their own home page. If children are just starting out, there's excellent information on general concepts like what the Internet is and the way files are exchanged between computers.

---

## Younger kids

---

*The early years are a crucial stage of children's intellectual development, and the Internet can be a great way to stimulate their interest – and make sure they get to grips with those all-important computer skills while they're young.*

**Ask Jeeves for Kids**                      **www.ajkids.com**
Essentially the same search engine as its big brother, this is the only site currently offering a search facility specifically aimed at kids. AJK takes children directly to a site selected as an appropriate answer to their question.

**Early Child Educators**                    **http://users.sgi.net/**
**and Family Web Corner**                    **~cokids**
This self-styled 'index to all things early childhood' is a richly informative destination for teachers and parents of young children.

The news section has the latest early childhood news, while other articles cover everything from brain research to the importance of play.

**EarlyChildhood**                    www.earlychildhood.com
Teachers: are you tired of repeating the same old projects year after year? Need a different Arts and Crafts idea for your classroom? This site has a huge range of stimulating teaching ideas for kindergarten classes, each conveniently grouped by subject.

**Gareth Pitchford's**                www.primaryresources.
**Primary Resources**                 co.uk
Aimed at teachers of children aged five to eleven – though most of the site is more applicable to the older section of the site's age range. Contains a useful bank of free, ready to use ideas, classroom resources, worksheets and lesson plans.

**The Infant Explorer**               www.naturegrid.org.uk/infant
A nicely designed literacy site designed for younger children. It aims to help them become confident and competent Internet users, encouraging them to use email and post their work to be published on the site.

**Kids @ National Geographic** www.nationalgeographic.com/kids
Kids will find this interactive site a fun place to research school projects. Of most use is the Archive, which indexes all articles dating back to 1996. Unfortunately there's no way to directly search these articles here – try a general search through www.nationalgeographic.com.

**Preschool Education**               www.preschooleducation.com
Amateur-looking site that is nevertheless packed with themed activities for the US kindergarten classroom. A handy parents guide to developmental milestones gives an idea what to expect from children of different ages.

**Underfives**                        www.underfives.co.uk
Free learning resources, practical information and help to teachers

and parents of children aged 1-4. There is useful material on early learning goals and advice on nurseries, pre-schools and playgroups.

## Homework and revision help

*Nobody likes homework – or so the theory goes. But if kids use the Internet to do it, even exam revision can become fun.*

### A-levels.co.uk                    www.a-levels.co.uk

This well organised destination is a useful source of links for various courses. Click on your chosen subject and a relevant page of links will pop up. There's advice for anyone thinking of taking a gap year and tips on what to expect from Oxford & Cambridge interviews.

### Bitesize Revision          www.bbc.co.uk/education/revision

The original UK revision site is still the best, covering the full range of GCSE and Scottish Standard Grade subjects. There is a subject-by-subject revision guide, broad content and a series of enjoyable test-yourself sections that help kids learn at their own pace.

### BJ Pinchbeck                      www.bjpinchbeck.com

Since April 1996, BJ and his dad have found hundreds of links to educational sites that they think kids will find useful – and created one of the most popular US homework sites. They've now teamed up with www.discoveryschool.com to offer more depth on the site.

### Digital Brain                     www.digitalbrain.co.uk

Subject-based tutored guides, exercises and links to the best sites compiled by teachers and linked to the UK National Curriculum – with the facility for students to keep notes online.

### GCSE Answers                           www.gcse.com

Poorly designed site that nevertheless has high-quality content, providing solid GCSE exam help, although only for English and mathematics.

**HomeWork Elephant**  www.homeworkelephant.co.uk
One of the best homework resources, offering lots of sites to research school topics and online help from the site's Agony Elephant. Pulls all the best homework helpers into one place.

**Homework Central**  www.homeworkcentral.com
Another compilation of links, but a good one. There are more than 100,000 links here in over 10,000 categories, all housed in an easy-to-use, safe environment.

**Homework Help**  www.homeworkhelper.co.uk
The bright and colourful homepage looks like a particularly messy child's bedroom – making it a familiar environment for kids to learn in. Click on anything in it to uncover associated links: so the Bible, for example, takes you to information about Religious Studies.

**Homework Help from About.com**  http://homeworkhelp.about.com
This guide includes tips to help you study more efficiently, write better reports, and approach exams without fear. There are also logical guides to finding the best online sites for all your school-related topics.

**Homework High**  www.homeworkhigh.com
Experienced teachers respond to homework headaches in this well-designed site from the UK's Channel 4. The huge searchable library has answers to more than 10,000 previously submitted questions.

**Homework Solver**  www.homeworksolver.com
Picture-heavy but professional offering promises to take the work out of homework. Arranged by school year groups, the site offers a series of subject tests to increase confidence.

**Kids Domain**  www.kidsdomain.co.uk
This user-friendly site contains hundreds of downloadable files – including software and pictures – as well as reviews of the latest educational software on the market.

**The Knowledge Adventure Encyclopedia  www.letsfindout.com**
A great homework helper for kids, helping them to access lots of well-presented information on an excellent range of subjects. Best of all, you can be sure that your kids are getting information that is safe.

**Please SIR**                                          **www.please-sir.co.uk**
UK based online tuition service for all subjects and ages (including GCSE, A-level, degree and adult learners) from carefully screened tutors who hold relevant UK qualifications.

**Revise.it**                                                  **www.revise.it**
Created by two Open University students, this site covers nine GCSE subjects and provides a good range of exam help. Although a little hit-and-miss, each topic is usefully broken down into subsections so students can focus their revision.

**Sam Learning**            **www.samlearning.co.uk/examrevision**
Thousands of questions covering all major exam subjects. Clever programming means that as you complete tests and exam papers online the site will record your marks for you and remember which sections you have already covered.

**Schoolzone**                                        **www.schoolzone.co.uk**
Easy access to Internet material for teachers, students and parents, without anyone trying to sell them anything or exploit them in any way. Despite the fiddly navigation system, this is an excellent jumping off point.

**Study Web**                                            **www.studyweb.com**
Vast directory of educational websites that provides links to topics such as architecture, literature and science. The site includes ratings by grade level and notes whether visual aids are available – useful if you're having to illustrate your lessons.

**Tutoring.co.uk**                                      **www.tutoring.cwc.net**
Provides a large directory of private tuition available in every UK

region with tips on finding a tutor and advice on expected costs. There is no mention of how they guarantee the credentials of the tutor, so parental caution is advisable.

## //SCHOOL SUBJECTS

*A selection of key sites in each subject to get you or your kids started. They won't necessarily be able to answer all your questions, but they will be able to point you to other sites that can.*

---

### Art

**ADAM**      http://adam.ac.uk
A big catalogue of digital art, design, architecture and media resources.

**Art History Resources**      http://witcombe.
**on the Web**      sbc.edu/ARTHLinks.html
Extensive directory of links arranged by period, including prehistoric, ancient, the Middle Ages, Baroque, and the 18th, 19th, and 20th centuries. Covers non-European works, prints and photography, and museums and galleries worldwide.

**The Mother of all**      www.umich.edu/~hartspc
**Art History Links**      /histart/mother
Ambitious title, and an excellent place to begin online art research. A huge number of reviewed links to art research sites and online image collections, and information on books and journals.

**Period and Style**      www.tulane.edu/lester/
**for Designers**      text/lester.html
Despite its dull homepage this is a great destination for anyone interested in art and architecture. A selection of high-quality images are accompanied by concise explanatory text. The site covers everything from ancient Egypt onwards.

**World Wide Arts Resources**                    http://wwar.com
Offers a comprehensive gateway to arts information and culture on the Internet – artists, museums, galleries, art history, arts education, antiques and performing arts ranging from dance to opera.

---

## Classics

**AncientWorld Web**                    http://julen.net
These info-packed pages focus on the latest articles, features, and other ephemeral aspects of the people, places, and objects of the ancient world. Most of the articles are reproduced from the popular press, so don't come here looking for dry academic discourse.

**The Classics Pages**                    www.classicspage.com
Over 500 encyclopedic pages of news, information, games and controversy covering the life, literature, art and archaeology of the ancient world. The 'Oracle' answers any query you might have.

**The Greeks: Crucible**                    www.pbs.org/
**of Civilisation**                    empires/thegreeks
Elegant, interactive timelines and a zooming map of Athens offer links to a range of material from architecture and politics to warfare. The audio presentation of the ancient Greek alphabet is especially interesting.

**Hellas:Net An exploration**                    http://monolith.yawc.net/
**of Ancient Greece**                    ~marsares
Although this site is still a work in progress, it remains one of the Internet's best sources of information on the ancient Greeks. Of the completed sections, history and warfare stand out for their huge range of material and authoritative tone.

**Roman Emperors**                    www.roman-emperors.org
Online encyclopedia of the rulers of the Roman Empire from Augustus to Constantine XI. Consists of an index of all the emperors who ruled during the empire's 1,500 years, biographical essays and maps of the empire at different times.

## English

### The English Institute      http://62.6.162.42/

Not the best-looking of sites, but this destination does a good job explaining the basics of English grammar. Actually designed for foreign students, its clarity and simplicity makes it an ideal place for kids to become acquainted with their own language.

### English Resources      www.englishresources.co.uk

Looking remarkably like Amazon.com, this UK site covers a broad range of learning materials for revising English at GCSE and A level. Useful for students needing extra assistance and teachers alike.

### The English Server      www.eserver.org

Put on your square hornrims and adopt a quizzical squint before accessing this brilliantly organised site that offers nearly 30,000 works online. They're grouped into 42 collections on themes such as contemporary art, race, 18th-century literary criticism, Internet studies, drama, gender studies and current political and social issues.

### Learning Network      www.nytimes.com/learning

Set up by the New York Times, this is a free service for students, their teachers and parents. English is brought to life by 'News Snapshots' that explore current events through NYT photos and text.

### Mr William Shakespeare      http://daphne.palomar.edu/
### and the Internet      shakespeare

A vast annotated guide to Shakespeare online. As well as the scholarly stuff, the site revisits theories about his death, including speculation that it followed a 'merry meeting' with his great contemporary, poet and dramatist Ben Jonson.

### Word Central      www.wordcentral.com

Award-winning US site with all sorts of useful features designed to make learning fun and help children build up their knowledge of the English language.

## Flags and facts

**CIA Factbook**   www.odci.gov/cia/publications/factbook
Created as an annual summary and update for spooks, this is now one of the best sources of country information available. Very well researched, and given the size of the Pentagon's defence budget, it will probably remain so.

**How Stuff Works**   www.howstuffworks.com
The average Western child has access to technology inconceivable a century ago, but do they understand how these wonders of modern life work? Explains how the news appears on TV, how phones work and more with logical prose and visual explanations.

**InfoNation**   www.un.org/Pubs/CyberSchoolBus/infonation
View and compare the most up-to-date statistical data for all the member states of the United Nations.

**The World Flag Database**   www.flags.net
Flags 'R' Us, covering all the world's countries and international organisations. Each page contains basic information including formal name, capital city, area, population, currency, languages, and religions.

## Geography

**EnviroLink**   www.envirolink.org
Brings together hundreds of organisations around the world to create an essential jumping-off point to environmental issues and news. The easily-navigable library is particularly useful.

**Get Mapping**   www.millennium-map.com
For a small fee, everyone can purchase an aerial photograph of their choice – from a view of their own street to London's Buckingham Palace. An exciting educational device for UK schools and universities.

**The Geographic Learning Site**      http://geography.state.gov

Learn all about the US Department of State. Includes profiles of interesting countries where US diplomats work, geographic hot spots and cool sites and the burning international issues of the day.

**Ordnance Survey**      www.ordsvy.gov.uk

A wealth of information about map reading, land use and more for teachers and students. Maps can be searched for by postcode or grid reference. There's a useful mapping search engine at www.landsurveyors.com.

**The Web of Culture**      www.webofculture.com

General geographic and social education on foreign nations and cultures, including information on food, currency, languages and religions.

---

## History

---

**British History**      http://britannia.com/history

The best British History resource on the Internet is, strangely enough, an American site. Features timelines, narrative histories, original source documents and important texts, biographies, maps, glossaries and reading lists.

**Internet History Sourcebooks Project**  www.fordham.edu/halsall

A complete set of collections of online historical texts, maps, and articles on a wide variety of subjects. Includes ancient, medieval, women's and modern history sections.

**Public Record**      http://learningcurve.pro.gov.uk/
**Office Snapshots**      snapshots

A showcase for a selection of the British PRO's landmark documents, using archive material to illuminate the past. The millennium exhibitions begin with the 11th-century Domesday book and use important documents to trace the history of the last 1,000 years.

**This Day in History**                    www.historychannel.com/today
A great way to stimulate interest in history every day of the year. Enter any date (today, a birthday, or whatever) to find out an historical anniversary to be marked.

**Top 100 Stories**                          www.usatoday.com/
**of the Century**                    2000/general/gen007.htm
A list of great headlines of the 20th century compiled by a survey of journalists and historians, with links to more information. There is an unavoidable US bias.

**The Victorian**                    http://landow.stg.brown.edu/
**Web**                              victorian/victov.html
Brilliant site covering the Victorian period (1830-1900) in tremendous depth, with an immense sweep covering politics, society and the expansion of Empire. Sub-sites cover every imaginable aspect of 19th century life, from the Great Exhibition of 1851 to the Boer War.

---

## Mathematics

---

**The Constants and Equations Pages**        http://tcaep.co.uk
Within this site you can look at over 550 scientific equations and constants. There are special sections for algebra, differentiation, trigonometry, integration and many other topics.

**Glossary of Mathematical Mistakes**    www.mathmistakes.com
Entertaining list of mathematical mistakes repeatedly made by advertisers, the media and politicians, designed to draw attention to the importance of maths in everyday life. The extensive archive beefs up the site's value as a research destination.

**MathsNet**                www.anglia.co.uk/education/mathsnet
Lots of useful ideas for learning maths and numerical skills, and a good starting place with links to other useful maths sites. There are also articles on different aspects of teaching the subject.

**Top Maths** www.topmaths.com

Mathematical puzzles and investigations for primary aged children, with free worksheets, activity ideas, lesson plans and more for parents and teachers. There are also suggestions for special needs teaching.

**Totally Tessellated** http://library.thinkquest.org/16661

A tessellation is any repeating pattern of interlocking shapes. This highly informative and fun introduction has background on the use and history of tessellation and a vibrant series of images.

---

## Science

**The MAD Scientist Network** www.madsci.org

Unites 800 scientists from around the world in one place where visitors learn more and ask questions. Physics, astronomy, engineering, computer science and the biological sciences are all well covered.

**Nature** www.nature.com

Browse past and present issues of Nature magazine – essential reading for all scientists – for the latest articles

**New Scientist** www.newscientist.com

An excellent resource for researching every aspect of science. It contains both general interest articles and in-depth treatment of highly technical subjects. The site will be of most use to older school kids and students.

**ScienceNet** www.sciencenet.org.uk

Similar database to the MAD network (see above), with questions addressed to a panel of UK scientists. All subjects, including engineering, technology and medicine, are covered and new questions and answers are added each month.

**The Why Files** http://whyfiles.news.wisc.edu

This site provides accurate and often droll explanations of the science and technology that underlie the news of the day. From the how-to of cloning to the hidden secrets of mosquitoes, science is made accessible to the public.

## //GOVERNMENT SITES

*There are a number of excellent government sites designed to help parents find out more about their children's education, health and welfare.*

**DfEE Parent Site**                    www.parents.dfee.gov.uk
Explains the assessments your child takes and matters such as school meals, security and uniform issues. Has details on health and welfare issues, plus information and advice for pre-school children and those seeking to move into further or higher education.

**Education Resource**                    www.ed.gov/
**Organizations Directory**                    Programs/EROD
Identify and contact US organisations that provide information and assistance on a broad range of education-related topics. In most cases there is a link directly to the organisation's home page.

**Federal Resources for Education Excellence**    www.ed.gov/free
Brings together hundreds of excellent education sites created by agencies across the US Federal government, including informative arts, foreign language and science sites.

**National Curriculum Online**                    www.nc.uk.net
What British schoolchildren must learn, and the attainment levels they are supposed to reach. Useful, detailed information on what the teachers expect.

**Ofsted**                    www.ofsted.gov.uk
Britain's school inspectors publish full primary and secondary school reports here. You can search for schools in a particular area or get information on a specific school.

# //CHOOSING A SCHOOL

*Deciding where your children go to school can influence where you choose to live. Use the Internet to make your search that little bit easier.*

**Boarding Schools**  www.boardingschools.hobsons.com
An online guide that helps you search for a UK school by area, age group or educational policy. Once you've found one that sounds suitable you can arrange for a prospectus to be sent to you, by snail mail.

**DfEE Parent Guide**  www.parents.dfee.gov.uk
An excellent search facility that lets you search the Department of Education and Employment school performance tables, school website database and Ofsted school reports databases in one fell swoop.

**Independent Schools Information Service**  www.isis.org.uk
Comprehensive guide to independent education in the UK, with details of 1,300 schools. The whacking fees specified are, believe it or not, termly – not annual.

**National Public**  http://nces.ed.gov/
**School Locator**  ccdweb/school
Lets you find the correct name, address, telephone number, NCES ID number and other important information for US public schools. There's a mirror site for private schools at **http://nces.ed.gov/surveys/pss/locator**.

**School Choices**  www.schoolchoices.org
Includes the latest statistics comparing the US public school system to free market alternatives based on vouchers, tax-credits and privatisation.

# //HIGHER EDUCATION AND ACADEMIC RESEARCH

*The web emerged from academia, so whatever your research topic, the Internet puts you in touch with other people in your field and offers the chance to search for published material around the world.*

## Starting points

**Academic Info**                    www.academicinfo.net

Austere, but clean and uncluttered subject directory of useful university-level resources on the net. This easily navigable gateway is probably the single best introduction to the range of online educational research.

**The Arts and Humanities Data Service**        http://ahds.ac.uk

UK service that integrates online catalogues of paper-based and digital information.

**Bath Information and Data Service**        www.bids.ac.uk

The best known and most widely used bibliographic service for the British academic community. You must register to use the service.

**Books for Academics**                www.ex.ac.uk/bfa

A valuable tool for academics and students researching published material in their disciplines. Links listed under subject headings will take the user directly to the relevant subject page in the publisher catalogue.

**British Education Index**            www.leeds.ac.uk/bei

Index to contents of 300 education and training journals, together with internationally published periodicals, national reports and conference literature.

**BUBL Information Service**            www.bubl.ac.uk

This service was originally set up to provide a bulletin board for academic librarians. It still does this, but it also caters for the whole academic and research community.

**The Chronicle of Higher Education**  http://chronicle.com
News for US college and university faculty members and administrators. Subscribers to the magazine who register receive free access to the site and regular email news updates.

**Critical Thinking**  www.philosophy.unimelb.edu.au/
**on the Web**  reason/critical
The University of Melbourne presents links to the most useful criticism sites on the web. Covers everything from cults and quackery to scepticism.

**The Data Archive**  www.data-archive.ac.uk
The largest collection of data in the social sciences and humanities in the UK. Through this site it is also possible to search the catalogues of other national archives.

**Edinburgh Data and**  http://edina.ed.ac.uk/
**Information Access**  index.shtml
EDINA provides online research services for UK tertiary education and research institutions free of charge.

**Infomine**  http://infomine.ucr.edu
Hugely comprehensive selection of websites collated by the University of California for students and research staff at university level. The best place to find databases, electronic journals, e-books, bulletin boards, online library catalogues, articles and directories of researchers.

**Ingenta.com**  www.ingenta.com
Free searching of over a million articles from professional and specialist articles, from thousands of online journals. Subscribers can view the full text with no extra charge; non-subscribers can access about half of the articles on a pay-per-view basis.

**Lectures Online**  www.lecturesonline.org
Handy for the lazy lecturer, this site collects and offers syllabi, lecture notes, and teaching materials from courses in a range of

disciplines. You can browse for materials in six categories or search by keyword.

**Link Environmental and**      **www.scotlink.org/**
**Academic Research Network**      **learn**
A unique two-way service offering students a choice of 'real life' research projects for environmental organisations that can be done as part of their academic coursework.

**Professionals for Professionals**      **www.mth.uea.ac.uk/vl**
Experts research and provide lists of key websites in their areas. Especially useful for the less than totally web-savvy academic who wants to stay in touch.

**Prospect Web**      **www.prospects.csu.ac.uk**
Database of postgraduate courses and research in the UK, with details of more than 5,000 research opportunities and advice on postgraduate funding. You can also arrange for updates to be sent to you by email.

**The Resource Discovery Network**      **www.rdn.ac.uk**
Excellent entry point to a full range of Internet, bibliographic, documentary and data resources.

**The Scout Report**      **www.scout.cs.wisc.edu/report/sr/**
These guys scout around for new Internet sites of interest to researchers, and publish their findings both on the web and by email. A very convenient way to keep abreast of developments.

**Science Technology Network**      **http://stneasy.cas.org**
Scientific information network that provides access to more than 200 databases from the world's leading scientific organisations. The best way to search for scientific literature or patents.

**The Social Science Information Gateway**      **http://sosig.ac.uk**
High-quality stuff for researchers and practitioners in the social sciences, business and law. The online database has thousands of high-quality, directly accessible sites.

**The Times Educational Supplement**      **www.thesis.**
**Educational Service**      **co.uk**
Subscribing to the paper edition will grant you access to an archive containing back issues from October 1994. The site also has good higher education links, including research assessments and teaching quality listings.

**Uncover**      **http://uncweb.carl.org**
Brief descriptive information of nearly nine million articles that have appeared in US journals since mid-1988. When you've found a likely-looking piece, you can ask them to fax you a copy.

**The Universities Advertising Group**      **www.jobs.ac.uk**
This is the dedicated recruitment website for the UK academic community. All kinds of teaching and research posts at universities, institutions of research and higher education, schools and colleges.

## //UNIVERSITIES

**All About College**      **www.allaboutcollege.com**
Thousands of links to colleges and universities around the world, including admissions office email addresses for most schools.

**Association of Universities**      **www.aucc.ca/en**
**and Colleges of Canada**
A list of Canadian universities arranged by geographical location or alphabetically. As well as direct links to the home pages, they also provide a brief description of the university.

**Braintrack**      **www.braintrack.com**
This beautifully simple site is a worldwide index of higher education institutions.

**CollegeBound Network**      **www.collegebound.com**
Helps high school students through the complicated college selection and application process, providing prospective students with first-hand information from those who have already experienced it.

**College Opportunities Online**　　http://nces.ed.gov/ipeds/cool
Direct links to over 9,000 colleges and universities in the US.

**CollegeView**　　www.collegeview.com
This excellent portal has sections on financial aid, careers, résumé writing, and preparing for interviews, as well as an easily searchable database of all accredited colleges and universities in the US and Canada.

**Degrees UK**　　www.degrees.ukf.net
A guide to UK degrees and life at university, packed with information for prospective students. There's also lots of help anyone looking for book and library details.

**TheGoodGuides**　　www.thegoodguides.com.au
Detailed descriptions of every campus in Oz and the low-down on every course – costs, admission requirements and specialisations.

**National Union of Students**　　www.nus.org.uk
Advice and up-to-the-minute education news for British students. Lots of useful information on fees, loans and managing your money with the help of a special budget calculator.

**The PUSH Guide to Which University**　　www.push.co.uk
Unbiased, no-nonsense reviews of all the universities in the UK. Includes links to university, student union and student-run websites for the official and unofficial view from the ground.

**StudentZone**　　www.studentzone.org.uk
This constantly-expanding UK site offers information for all students, including helpful links for your discipline.

**University and College Admission Scheme**　　www.ucas.ac.uk
The central organisation that processes all Britain's undergraduate applications. The course search is designed as an initial guide to courses offered by higher education institutions in the UK. The site comes into its own every August as students scramble to find places in the clearing process.

**University Map** www.scit.wlv.ac.uk/ukinfo
This map shows all recognised universities, university colleges and higher education colleges in the UK. Click on it to be taken to the university's own website.

**UK Course Discover** www.ecctis.co.uk
Strives to match people with the best possible academic environment. Course Discover is the largest database in the UK and includes over 100,000 courses.

**Which University** www.whichuni.hobsons.com
Key information about all universities and colleges of higher education in the UK, searchable by subject or location. View extensive profiles of more than 180 institutions.

## //LIBRARIES

**Association of Research Libraries** www.arl.org
The leading research libraries in North America unite to show off some of the finest scholarly resources in the world.

**The Berkeley Digital Library SunSITE** http://sunsite.berkeley.edu
Builds some of the world's most extensive digital collections, while supporting digital library developers worldwide.

**Blaise** http://blaiseweb.bl.uk
The British Library's Automated Information Service, providing access to 21 databases containing over 18.5 million bibliographic records. That's a lot of books.

**British Library** www.bl.uk
Access the BL's major collections via the web.

**EARL** www.earl.org.uk
Consortium of British public libraries provides a useful ready-made collection of bookmarks designed to help you find your way around the Internet. You can also ask a librarian to help you with your query.

**Gabriel**  http://portico.bl.uk/gabriel
Central point for Europe's national libraries – currently 40 libraries from 38 states take part. Plenty of information about the libraries, their collections and their services.

**High Wire Press**  http://highwire.stanford.edu
One of the largest archives of free full-text science research on Earth. At the time of writing, this site was publishing 676,932 articles online.

**The Internet Public Library**  www.ipl.com
The traditional library reinvented for the digital age. The excellent service includes 'Pathfinders' – guides written by IPL staff to help you start your research.

**The Library Association**  www.la-hq.org.uk
British librarians use their expertise to answer enquiries by email.

**Library of Congress**  http://lcweb.loc.gov
The access point for 119 million items, including the largest map, film and television collections in the world.

**LibrarySpot**  www.libraryspot.com
Brings the best library and reference sites together in a valiant attempt to tackle the web's information overload.

**OCLC**  www.oclc.org
Delivers online reference information through a rich collection of databases with links to full text versions, electronic journals and library holdings.

**UK Higher Education**  www.ex.ac.uk/
**and Research Libraries**  library/uklibs.html
Lists more than 150 libraries and information services, including those of universities, university colleges, and institutes and colleges of higher education.

## Newsgroups

**alt.education.alternative** – school doesn't have to suck

**alt.education.higher** – higher education discussion

**alt.education.research** – studying about studying

**alt.education.university** – college chat

**comp.edu** – computer science education

**k12.chat.teacher** – conversation for teachers of grades K-12

**k12.ed.science** – science curriculum in K-12 education

**k12.ed.special** – US special needs education

**uk.education.governors** – news for UK governors

**uk.education.maths** – problems with sums

**uk.education.staffroom** – teachers compare notes

**uk.education.teachers** – discussion for and about teachers

# 6//BUSINESS RESEARCH

The Internet gives professionals the chance to stay on top at work, and many business people now cannot imagine doing their job without using email or accessing the web for company analysis, detailed market research, up-to-the-minute stock details or comprehensive background on a market or company. The Internet brings the best-stocked business library on Earth into your office. Whatever type of business you are in, however broad or specialised your market, you will find it makes your working life easier.

What's more, a lot of today's business revolves around the Internet itself. Wired-up businessmen are driving what's often called 'the new economy', with the power to transform working patterns, careers and lifestyles. Even if they're not fully-fledged dotcoms, most businesses have an Internet presence. Those that don't are listed in various Internet directories, so you can use the net to find out basic information about nearly every company.

More than ever, information is the lifeblood of business. If you're relying on old technology for your facts and figures then you'll never keep up with the wired entrepreneurs. If you don't keep up, you're out of business.

In this chapter you'll find market research, extensive company information, small business advice and the latest news, whether hi-tech or old money. But if you want to find out more, there are exhaustive listings and wide-ranging advice in **The Virgin Internet Business Guide**.

## //ADDRESS BOOK

**Starting points**

| | |
|---|---|
| **BizProLink Network** | **www.bizprolink.com** |

The leading US Business-to-Business (B2B) e-commerce research destination. Although it will never win prizes for good design, the network of B2B industry-specific sites (124 at the time of writing) is hugely impressive. Each sub-site functions as a home page and vital 'first-point-of-contact' for those in the same industry.

**Brainwave**                                    www.brainwave.telebase.com
Owned by Office.com, Brainwave is a pay-as-you-go destination for mainly US business information such as company profiles, credit reports, trademarks, patents, market research and industry news.

**Brint**                                                    www.brint.com
It ain't pretty, but this mass of text links has been described as the Yahoo! for e-business and technology. It's all in here somewhere.

**Business Information Resources**              www.bird-online.
**for the UK and Ireland**                                    co.uk
This extensive site offers easy access to detailed business information. Use the industry-specific search engines or download concise and authoritative overviews of a particular market straight to your desktop, for as little as £10 each.

**Business Information**                          www.dis.strath.
**Sources on the Internet**                        ac.uk/business
Excellent selective list of useful online business information sources on the Internet. The high quality of the links makes this one of the best places to start your research.

**Companies House**                        www.companieshouse.gov.uk
The fount of all knowledge for UK companies. This official body holds information on over 1.5 million registered companies and files more than 5 million documents each year. For an initial fee of £50, a £7.50 a month subscription and a range of other costs (depending on what you want to view) you can find out about shareholders, look up past results and more.

**The Department of Trade and Industry**              www.dti.gov.uk
Another UK government site offering excellent information for businesses and employees. Whether you are looking for hard facts

on the aerospace or biotech industries or guidance on the latest regulations, there's a good chance this site will be able to help.

### Dialogweb                                                  www.dialogweb.com

Probably the most impressive business research site of them all, Dialog provides a hugely powerful, subscription-only method to search thousands of authoritative business, scientific, intellectual property and technical publications. Financial information on 14 million companies is just the start: the site also contains the complete text of more than 200 newspapers and access to all the major wire services around the world. The complicated price structure comes as a printable 54-page document.

### Dun & Bradstreet                                                  www.dnb.com

Get the lowdown on more than businesses in 200 countries from one of the biggest holders of company information in the world. D&B offer extensive material covering a company's history, financial performance and market position. For a UK focus, try the sister site at **www.dunandbrad.co.uk**. Either way, you will probably have to pay a fee for any serious data.

### The Enterprise Zone                                      www.enterprisezone.org.uk

First port of call for many a small businessman, the EZ only carries material deemed relevant to small and medium-sized enterprises.

### EuroPages                                                  www.europages.com

Huge directory with over half a million company addresses from 30 European countries, access to key business information and links to yellow pages. Search by product or service, by activity sector or company name – in six languages.

### FT.com                                                          www.ft.com

The new media counterpart of the *Financial Times* is a world-class analyser of financial markets, industries and companies. Sure, there's all the stuff you would expect from a newspaper – industry news, insights from FT commentators and news on the people behind the headlines. But there's also easy access to extensive online business directories and answers to your business questions in an open collection of over 3,500 publications. The business directory at **http://search.ft.com/directory/topLevelNavigation.htm** has 27,000 key URLs of the best online business information available.

### Hoovers                                      www.hoovers.com

Exhaustive material on companies, industries and people. Essential reading if you're pursuing sales leads, checking out a competitor, researching an attractive investment, or just hunting for business news. Hoovers UK (**www.hoovers.co.uk**) offers an anglocentric slant, with a special focus on companies in the FTSE 100 and FTSE 250.

### IKnowUK                                      www.knowuk.co.uk

A quiet gem, this site draws together authoritative reference materials (most of which you can't get freely elsewhere on the Internet) to provide key information on key UK people, institutions and organisations.

### LEXIS-NEXIS                                   www.lexis-nexis.com

A trusted source of business information for 26 years. Search fees start at £9 a document, and there is a vast range of useful information here for anyone in business.

### US Business Advisor                           www.business.gov

A government-backed central point of access to the 60+ different federal organisations that assist or regulate business. There's a good business resource library here, too.

---

### News

---

*Some of these sites only offer their full service to subscribers, but there is always enough free information to make them useful newsgathering destinations.*

**BBC Business News**     http://news.bbc.co.uk/hi/english/business
Market movements, London share prices, foreign exchange rates and other financial news and comment. Lots of links to additional material – much of it on sites outside the BBC – and free access to the site's huge archive.

**Bloomberg**                                    www.bloomberg.com
Superbly organised site from the internationally respected Bloomberg financial news service, providing reliable up-to-the-minute news and information.

**Business Week**                            www.businessweek.com
Subscribers to the magazine can search the past five years' worth of issues for free. Otherwise there is a fee-based archive for stories dating back to January 1991.

**Company News**                            www.companynews.co.uk
Lists research reports and comments and provides the latest data on UK quoted companies – including links to corporate sites and more detailed financial data.

**CNN Financial Network**                        www.cnnfn.com
One of the most useful financial portals, CNN's financial network has a wealth of information, particularly for US markets.

**The Economist**                              www.economist.co.uk
Registered users and subscribers to the printed version can scour the archives of this leading business weekly back to January 1995 for free. Otherwise, you can search and view headlines free of charge, though retrieving each article costs $1.

**Far Eastern Economic Review**                    www.feer.com
Hong Kong based FEER is the single best source of detailed information about Asian markets. There's free access to the magazine's archives and the yearly Review 200, the definitive regional survey.

**Forbes**                                        www.forbes.com
The archives contain *Forbes Magazine* publications back to 1996.

The site also includes Forbes' listing of The World's Richest People and The International 800 – Forbes' annual directory of multinational corporations.

**London Stock Exchange**  www.londonstockexchange.com
Constantly updated news on the performance of shares listed on the UK markets. Graph the progress of up to 10 securities, hoping the lines move up instead of down.

**Nasdaq**  www.nasdaq.com
Newswire feeds, portfolio tracking, and links to nearly 3,000 hi-tech companies are among this expensive-looking site's most popular functions.

**News Page**  www.newspage.com
Set up your own page with tailored business, trade and financial news all in one place. Choose daily news on thousands of industry topic areas and even elect to see press releases from over 15,000 companies.

**Nikkei**  www.nni.nikkei.co.jp
Sister site to the company's flagship newspaper, this hugely comprehensive site has everything about doing business with Japan, with incisive articles on economics, business, finance and politics.

**Research Index**  www.researchindex.co.uk
A database of headlines of news, views and comments on industries and companies worldwide, as reported in the UK national press and a range of quality business magazines.

**UK Business and**  www.news-review.
**Financial News Review**  co.uk
Comprehensive summary of business news from the quality UK weekend newspapers, which you can see here or have emailed to you every Sunday evening. Access the archive of back copies by company name back to June 1995.

**Wall Street Journal Interactive**       http://interactive.wsj.com
Contains breaking news affecting financial markets, corporations, business, and technology and features a personalised news alert for subscribers.

## Data & Reports

*Market research data is expensive to collect, so it's usually held in password-protected paying databases – but there's also a huge range of free information.*

**AC Nielsen**       www.acnielsen.com
Leading provider of market research, information and analysis.

**DeepCanyon**       www.deepcanyon.com
Strategic research, business tools, access to industry analysis and trends to help US marketeers to put together strategies and assess the competition.

**Demos**       www.demos.co.uk
Independent and influential think-tank and research institute based in London. Its findings can have major repercussions for business.

**Euromonitor**       www.euromonitor.com
Leading provider of global consumer market and business intelligence, publishing more than 400 market reports and 30 statistical reference handbooks every year. From this site you can access sections from their latest reports on a pay-per-view basis.

**Experian**       www.experian.com/uk/index.html
One of the world's leading suppliers of information on consumers, businesses, motor vehicles and property and an excellent place to research risk management.

**Gallup**       www.gallup.com
Ace pollsters Gallup use their expertise to help companies improve business performance. Extensive information on their research methods and contact details so you can find out more.

**Infonautics**                                    www.infonautics.com
A fast-growing online research provider, with easy-to-use services designed to give you the edge. The 'company sleuth' here keeps digging to uncover hard-to-get business information.

**IntelliQuest**                                   www.intelliquest.com
Marketing research for hi-tech industries, and the place where dotcommers come to track product performance, measure advertising effectiveness, assess brand strength and competitive position and evaluate new business opportunities.

**Market & Opinion Research International**        www.mori.com
Access to MORI's world class research services and contact details for its experts. There's a useful poll digest here with updates on a wide range of recent surveys.

**Market Research News**                           www.mrnews.com
An essential bookmark for all involved in market research. Get contact details for market research agencies or search the database for background information.

**Mintel**                                         www.mintel.co.uk
A leading publisher of consumer market research, with more than 400 reports each year examining every conceivable consumer market. After registration you can browse the entire range of reports.

**Perfect Information**                            www.perfectinfo.com
An impressive digital library of more than 1.4 million company documents, broken down into market and geographical sectors. The service is available on a pay-as-you-go basis or by subscription.

**World Investor Link**                            www.icbinc.com
At last, a convenient way for investors to get company annual reports. Let them know what you want, and they'll dig it out.

## Statistics

**Audit Bureau of Circulation**                    **www.abc.org.uk**
ABC audits circulation figures for more than 3,000 UK publications.
This site gives details of cover price and subscription rates as well.
Find out about their efforts to audit electronic publications at
www.abce.org.uk.

**Australian Bureau of Statistics**                **www.abs.gov.au**
AusStats is a web based information service providing you with the
ABS' full product range (both free and charged material) online. It
includes extensive economic and social data.

**The Central Office of Information**              **www.coi.gov.uk**
Among other things, the Orwellian-sounding COI is responsible for
supplying firms with detailed government information.

**Eurostat**                                       **http://europa.eu.int**
Easy access to official EU statistical information, most of which you
have to pay for.

**Organisation for Economic**                      **www.oecd.org**
**Co-operation and Development**
The Statistics Directorate collects and standardises economic
statistics from around the world and publishes them here in
electronic form.

**The Source**                                     **www.statistics.gov.uk**
A wide range of UK data under one umbrella. You can rely on
figures you get here – they're official.

**Statistics Canada**                              **www.statcan.ca**
The country's national statistical agency, organised into three broad
subject matter areas: demographic and social, socio-economic and
economic. This site provides free tabular data on Canada's
economy, land, people and government.

## Companies

*Most company websites have extensive profiles, including mission statements and profiles of the executives. If you're not satisfied by the party line, there's plenty of independent information, too.*

**aRMadillo UK Company Database**  **www.rmonline.com**
Instant access to full company search reports, credit analysis and director searches on over two million UK registered companies and non-limited businesses. The Trade Mark Database lets you search all UK and registered marks, complete with images of registered devices and logos.

**British Chamber of Commerce**  **www.britishchambers.org.uk**
Local organisations that support and campaign on behalf of firms in all sectors and of all sizes. Contact your local chamber through this site.

**Companies Online**  **www.companiesonline.com**
Popular joint venture between Lycos and Dun & Bradstreet that lets you search for a specific company by name or stock market ticker symbol. Designed like a standard directory, you can also locate businesses by category.

**Company Annual Reports Online**  **www.carol.co.uk**
Carol claims to be the world's biggest annual report site, providing direct links to 3,000 corporate reports drawn from Europe, Asia and America. The site searches more than 100 of the world's financial-news sources for company specific information.

**Equifax**  **www.infocheck.co.uk**
Credit information about two million UK companies, businesses and sole traders.

**Insolvency.co.uk**  **www.insolvency.co.uk**
The leading UK bankruptcy and insolvency website summarises the best Internet insolvency and bankruptcy links on one site, and carries official announcements and notices.

**Investex** www.investext.com

A leading source for global company and industry research. Reliable information with reports from analysts at firms such as Morgan Stanley Dean Witter, Merrill Lynch and Credit Suisse First Boston.

**Juniper** www.icc.co.uk

One of the fastest online business information services around, providing company analysis, original documents and searches for professional users.

**OneSource** www.onesource.com

Business and financial information on over a million public and private companies around the world, accessible at a fixed annual subscription price.

**Primark Financial Information Division** www.disclosure.com

Brings high-quality US financial information directly to your desktop.

**UK Data Ltd** www.ukdata.com

Holds full online credit reports and scanned copies of the latest accounts on every UK business. Full reports cost £18.

**UK Equities Direct** www.hemscott.com/equities

This service is free of charge, which has helped the site to become the most widely used source of information on fully listed and AIM companies.

---

## Markets

---

*Every major market in the world has a web presence. Simply try inserting the market's name into a popular search engine like www.google.com. Here are some of the major ones.*

**FTSE** www.ftse.com

FTSE devise and calculate the FTSE indices which are used as a barometer of the health of the London market. The site offers end-of-day trading information and a searchable database of sectors and companies.

**Lloyds**       **www.lloydsoflondon.co.uk**
Venerable Lloyds is the world's major insurance market. If you're planning to sail around the world or travel to a war zone, this site could help you to negotiate a suitable policy.

**Nasdaq**       **www.nasdaq.com**
If you want to try and inflate the next dotcom bubble, come to Nasdaq, which is still the most high-tech of trading markets. Look up share prices by company name or symbol.

**New York Stock Exchange**       **www.nyse.com**
Wall Street comes to the Web, with a special section for novice investors, easy access to market data and links to NYSE listed company websites.

**Tokyo Stock Exchange**       **www.tse.or.jp/eindex.html**
Market data and info on listed companies in Japan.

---

**Europe**

---

**Bundesbank**       **www.bundesbank.de/index_e.html**
Dour yet authoritative data from the Bundesbank, with information on the bank's many specialist departments. Also contains press releases – in German.

**Business Central Europe**       **www.bcemag.com**
Basic-looking site with a lot of useful information. The free statistical database provides annual historical data going back to 1990, searchable by country.

**Community Research and Development**       **www.cordis.lu**
**Information Service**
Luxembourg hosts the most extensive collection of EU-funded research available.

**EU Business** www.eubusiness.com

This excellent guide through the EU information maze offers fast and easy access to information about European legislation and policies.

**Eurochambres** www.eurochambres.be

Not a hotel booking service, but a continent-wide association of Chambers of Commerce and Industry which together represent over 14 million businesses.

**European Business Register** www.ebr.org

Official information on European businesses, without the language barrier.

**European Central Bank** www.ecb.int

Info-packed site with links to all the EU central banks and details of all the ECB's monetary policy decisions. There are Euro area statistics, daily exchange rates for the Euro and a sneak preview of the Euro banknotes.

**European Voice** www.european-voice.com

In-depth analysis of the most important developments in the EU. Once you've registered, you will be emailed any story which contains any keywords you set. Try not to include 'Europe' as one of your keywords.

---

**International**

---

**Asia-Pacific.com** www.asia-pacific.com

A first-class site – provided you can cope with, or switch off, the cheesy classical music. Analysis includes links to economic sources, company annual reports, and trade reports for the Asia-Pacific region.

**The Asia Web Guide** www.nni.nikkei.co.jp/FR/AWG

Excellent list of Asian companies that offer Internet sites in English. Companies and organisations can be browsed alphabetically or by country. Users can also search by descriptive keyword.

**British Exports**                    www.britishexports.com
Multi-lingual site with essential information on nearly 20,000 UK exporting companies.

**British Trade International**              www.brittrade.com
Official support for British traders and investors overseas, with advice on planning an export strategy.

**IMF/ World Bank Libraries**    http://jolis.worldbankimflib.org
The fourteen libraries that serve the World Bank and International Monetary Fund make some of their resources available to the public here.

**International**                      www.library.nwu.edu/
**Documents**                                govpub/
Huge directory of international organisations with websites.

**International Political**              http://csf.colorado.
**Economy Network**                          edu/ipe
Excellent mailing list bringing people together to discuss the global economy. Hot topics include regional trading blocs, international debt, currency and market crises and commodity negotiations.

**Middle East Business Information**         www.ameinfo.com
The leading provider of business information in the Middle East has exhaustive details of 200,000 companies in fourteen separate countries. Additional content includes an updated regional exhibition calendar, dialling codes, ISP index and travel information.

**Skate Financial Network**              www.skatefn.com
Details of hundreds of publicly traded companies in fourteen countries of emerging Europe. View the performance of financial indicators for equities, bonds and funds in the CEE and Russia.

**The World in 2000**                    www.theworldin.com
*The Economist* magazine's annual flagship publication attempts to predict the world's major political and business developments of the next year.

## E-commerce

*Understand the risks and opportunities of this dynamic new marketplace.*

**Business 2.0**                          **www.business2.com**

Despatches from the global electronic marketplace, telling you how technologies driving the engines of change really work, and how they could work for your business.

**Clnet**                                **www.cnet.com**

Exhaustive news for millions of users each day from the world's leading provider of technology information to the masses. Sign up and they'll email bulletins straight to your inbox.

**CyberAtlas**                   **http://cyberatlas.internet.com**

Statistics, marketing information and more for the wired generation.

**Encyclopedia of**                        **http://hotwired.**
**the New Economy**                            **lycos.com**

*Wired* magazine's guide to a world of constant, rapid change. A world in which people work with their brains instead of their hands. Which is why it gives you a headache.

**Forrester Research**                    **www.forrester.com**

The world's leading independent Internet research firm, focussing on how technological developments such as WAP, interactive TV, and broadband could affect businesses.

**Iconocast**                            **www.iconocast.com**

Award-winning mailing list delivers insightful reporting on news, analysis and trends affecting the Internet marketing industry – an essential read for e-commerce decision makers anywhere.

**Nua**                                  **www.nua.ie**

Come here for authoritative surveys of Internet demographics, statistics and trends, widely regraded as the oracle of future trends.

**New York Times Technology**             **www.nytimes.com/tech**
Breaking news, original features and articles from the newspaper –
and The New York Times Navigator – a guide to the net used by the
paper's own reporters.

**Red Herring**                           **www.redherring.com**
Impressive analysis and insider perspectives lend plenty of cred to
this site's commentary on hi-tech business. Trawl through the
business news and investment information for insights into the
latest events and trends.

**Silicon.com**                           **www.silicon.com**
Choose the news you're interested in and this leading online media
company will make sure you get it.

**The Standard**                          **www.thestandard.net**
All about the people, companies and business models shaping the
Internet economy. Find out how where the web traffic is, which
business models are working and how much money is being spent
on web advertising.

**Tasty Bits from the Technology Front**      **www.tbtf.com**
Industry favourite TBTF updates you by email to breaking e-
commerce news. It makes you sound like you know what you are
talking about, even if you don't.

**Time Digital**                          **www.time.com/time/digital**
An excellent source of smart, jargon-free tech news.

---

## Regulation & Tax

**Financial Services Authority**              **www.fsa.gov.uk**
The FSA maintains a register of firms currently or formerly
authorised to carry on investment business in the UK. You can
check it here.

**HM Customs & Excise**                   **www.hmce.gov.uk**
Keep up to date with taxes and duties with the vast array of info

supplied here. Did you know that this department brings in around 40 per cent of central government's total tax income?

**Inland Revenue** www.inlandrevenue.gov.uk
General information on UK income tax, VAT and National Insurance.

**The Regulation Home Page** www.regulation.org
Comprehensive source of regulatory studies, statistics, and information – the image of the Statue of Liberty wrapped in red tape gives you a good idea where the site's sympathies lie.

**Tax and Accountancy Sites Directory** www.taxsites.com
Goodness. What a comprehensive index of US tax and accounting sites. And what an excellent starting point for people who are searching for more information.

---

## Small Businesses

**Better Business Online** www.better-business.co.uk
Facts, vital contacts and moneymaking ideas for self-employed professionals, small business managers and startups.

**British Franchise** www.british-franchise.org.uk
General information for people contemplating business as a franchisee, companies considering becoming a franchiser – indeed, anyone wishing to investigate the world of franchising.

**Business Link** www.businesslink.co.uk
Lots of information for UK small businesses.

**Business Training Library** www.bizlibrary.com
Join this site's unique lending library and you can 'borrow' high-quality training materials from America's leading producers for as long as you want.

**The Federation of Small Business** www.fsb.org.uk
Excellent UK directory with an online trading service and free email newsletters.

**Information Society Initiative**  www.isi.gov.uk/isi
Impartial advice on using IT, with case studies, jargon busters and explanation of how government legislation affects small businesses.

**Live Wire**  www.shell-livewire.org
Pick up some great business advice and check out the ten most popular business ideas courtesy of this excellent site from Shell oil. Live Wire helps 16-30 year olds to start and develop their own business and hosts a national competition for new start-ups.

**Microsoft bCentral**  www.bcentral.com
Lots of useful stuff for small businesses, including technology guides and advice on improving your organisational skills.

**Small Business Administration**  www.sba.gov
America's 25 million small businesses employ more than half of the work force and generate more than half of the nation's GDP. This government site provides financial, technical and management assistance to help you start, run and grow your business.

**Small Business Knowledge Base**  www.bizmove.com
Hundreds of pages of practical information on topics such as personnel audits, cash flow management, marketing plans and cost-cutting.

**Small Business Service**  www.dti.gov.uk/sbs
The UK government organisation dedicated to the interests of small business.

**UK SME**  http://uk.sme.com
A good collection of business related links for small- and medium-sized enterprises in the UK. At the US sister site (www.sme.com) there's a 'WorldWide TradeCenter' where you can find business opportunities just about anywhere.

**ZDNET: Small Business**  www.zdnet.com/smallbusiness
This US site has logical step-by-step answers to the classic small business questions about planning, advertising, marketing and more.

## Business Finders

*Why waste time ringing round trying to find suppliers? Log on, click here and away you go.*

### Ask Alex                    www.askalex.co.uk

Directory of nearly two million UK businesses searchable by name, product, or location. Provides company contact information, addresses, and speciality services.

### BigYellow                    www.bigyellow.com

Let your fingers do the walking through 17 million US business listings and 100 million residential listings to discover postal addresses, phone numbers and email addresses. There's also information and advice on technology, home-office issues and more.

### The Biz Directory                    www.thebiz.co.uk

Aims to be a comprehensive listing of companies and business-to-business resources across the UK.

### FIND                    www.find.co.uk

Leading Internet directory for UK financial services. Search here for company websites. There are also links to debt management services and help arranging insurance.

### ThompsonWeb                    www.infospace.com/uk.thomw

Featuring over two million businesses, the Thomson database is the most comprehensive of its type in the UK. Identify businesses by key parameters such as company name, business type, location, postcode, number of employees.

### The UK Business Net                    www.ukbusinessnet.com

This site currently contains over 5,000 pages of free-access information on companies, trade news, forthcoming industrial and commercial events and trade and technical media.

## Newsgroups

**alt.business.internal-audit** – discussion of internal auditing

**alt.business.international** – cross-border business

**alt.business.import-export** – international trade

**alt.business.offshore** – all about tax havens

**alt.management** – how to run 'tings

**biz.accounting** – accountancy chat

**biz.control** – be your own boss

**scot.business.internet** – business highland style

**uk.business.accountancy** – discussion on accountancy products and services in UK

# 7//GENEALOGY

It's the newest of jungles, but the skills of the hunter-gatherers are being rediscovered as Internet users rush to find out about ancestors and far-flung families. Genealogy has become one of the most popular of all online activities.

One of the first things people most first-time Internet users do is type their name into a search engine. If you have an unusual name this can be a useful way of finding information, but this approach won't get you anywhere if your name is Smith or Jones – these will throw up thousands of references.

Luckily, it doesn't end there. There are myriad sites providing information on getting started with your genealogical research, finding your ancestors and networking with others who may be able to help. And the vast majority of genealogical data remains free.

Before the emergence of the net, genealogists had to spend a lot of time and money sending off requests for marriage licenses, birth certificates, death certificates and other records – and then wait months for a response. Today, the huge variety of genealogy resources on the Internet has slashed expectations of the time required to find information. The Internet isn't yet an online record office, though it will find indexes and records among its pages, so while the specific document or details may not be available online, a careful search can usually reveal where it is located.

### Fashionable and fun

Genealogy has not been this popular since the 16th century, when the English nobility had to prove that their family lines went back to the Norman Conquest of 1066. Hatfield House, in Hertfordshire, has a copy of a family tree which purports to trace Queen Elizabeth I's ancestors all the way back to Adam and Eve. You're unlikely to get that far, but the Internet makes it easier to trace your ancestors than ever before. Enthusiasts are united by a need to communicate across distances and to discover like-minded researchers.

Indeed, thanks to the Internet, a hobby once seen as bookish and dull has now become fashionable. Membership of the UK Society of Genealogists has doubled in a decade. The key to this explosion of interest is the way the Internet facilitates easy access to hitherto off-limits information.

Surprisingly, dot.com mania in the UK has not yet led to the launch of a big commercial genealogy portal along the lines of one of the American success stories. For anyone in the UK, this means that your search for information has to involve a fair bit of ingenuity and cunning – there is no central site to help you do everything. Where the net makes a huge difference to your search is in the positive sharing of information. Newsgroups and mailings lists provide information for groups of people searching for the same surname, and let you tap into the knowledge of anyone who has already covered the same ground you are embarking on.

The sense of camaraderie among genealogy researchers closely resembles the original spirit of the Internet – thriving on communication and beneficial co-operation. Family historians are keen collaborators, sharing findings and helping each other through the myriad complexities of historical research. Although there is much goodwill, sharing is also motivated by the calculated recognition that genealogical research is a complicated process on which many people are working simultaneously. Your next breakthrough could easily lie on someone else's PC.

**How to do it**
Before you start exploring sites there are some vital things to remember when you begin your research. The key to constructing a successful family tree is meticulous organisation and dogged persistence. Keep going even if the trail seems to have gone cold – your next lead is only a click away.

**Start offline** First, draw up as much of your family tree as you can, then ask relatives, especially parents and grandparents, to add to it. This provides you with a useful starting point and reference, as well as a partial history of your ancestors that could go back at least a hundred years. As well as throwing up some fascinating anecdotes (and perhaps a juicy scandal or two), there's a logic to tapping your family's collective memory. You are much more likely to find information about your great-great-grandfather MacLeod if you know his son Hector was born in Tobermory, Mull, in 1872, than if you start scouring all the online MacLeod surname databases when you're not even sure of your great-grandfather's first name or where he grew up.

In any case, you won't be able to track the entire history of your family on the Internet. Many physical records are not yet available online. In most countries these include birth, death and marriage certificates, census and military records. Although these are available for public scrutiny, they are usually on paper, which makes it difficult (and expensive) for them to be translated into electronic format.

**Check the obvious places** Next, try searching for a local genealogical society in an area where you believe your ancestors lived. There's a good chance they'll have a site, and, if they do, it should provide a lot of useful information.

Then try official sources. In the UK, the Office for National Statistics Family Records Centre in London (**www.ons.gov.uk/register/frc.htm**) has census returns from 1841, newspapers, and trade directories. The Principal Registry (also in London) has copies of wills going back to 1858.

Before civil records were kept, baptisms, marriages and funerals were entered in church registers. The Society of Genealogists (**www.sog.org.uk**) has the largest collection of copies. Anyone searching for lost relatives can leave a message under their family name on one of the popular genealogical websites for a possible email response. Sometimes all you need to do is key in a family name on an Internet search engine to open a promising trail.

Try a few search engines, but be as specific as possible. If you are researching a general topic, if you're searching for Aberdeen, Illinois, you'll quickly become annoyed if your search for genealogy AND aberdeen produces loads of genealogy links for Aberdeen, Scotland.

**Check your sources** Sorry, you can't do it all on your PC. Go back and check the original source – like the parish register – to ensure nothing has been lost in the translation to the web. Just because you find an Allan Arthur born in 1848, doesn't mean it is the right Allan Arthur, even if he is born in the right place and at the right time. There is nothing more frustrating than your hard-work being wasted by a case of mistaken identity.

## //ADDRESS BOOK

### Starting points

*There are thousands of websites devoted to genealogical research, providing a huge amount of information available online. After you've seen what a basic search on Altavista or Yahoo! throws up, you'll want to tap into the specialist sites, often run by enthusiastic amateurs.*

### UK & Ireland Genealogical Information Service
www.genuki. org.uk

The best starting point from a British point of view is the non-commercial Genuki. Both a guide to British genealogy and a vast series of links, Genuki isn't pretty, but crucially it works.

On the whole, the information provided on Genuki relates to primary historical material such as cemetery, land, property and population information. Its role is thus very different from Internet-based services such as GenServ, Roots Surname List and the **soc.genealogy.surnames.britain** and **soc.genealogy.surnames.ireland** newsgroups, which help genealogists to find others researching the same family and share their results. These services are reviewed later in this chapter.

The structure of this huge site is based closely on the method used by the Mormon Family History Library in Salt Lake City, which is the largest genealogy library in existence. The British site offers a chance to establish which resources are available in any given public record office or library, and provides thousands of links to the services offered by family history societies around Britain and overseas.

The principal means of structuring is a four-level hierarchy based on locality, which reflects the way major archives and official records are organised. The top level covers the British Isles as a whole. The next consists of England, Ireland, Scotland, Wales, the Channel Islands and the Isle of Man (Ireland here covers both the Republic of Ireland and Northern Ireland). The third level of the hierarchy corresponds to counties and the fourth corresponds to towns and parishes.

There's also information on a huge range of subjects ranging from almanacs to yearbooks, including emigration and immigration, heraldry, military records and postal and shipping guides.

**Cyndi's List**                                    **www.cyndislist.com**
Comprehensive and well-organised coverage of all aspects of the subject has made this the most popular genealogy portal on the Internet. The site has more than 65,000 links, categorised into over 120 subject areas.

Begin with the huge, categorised and cross-referenced index to genealogical resources on the Internet. This is a list of links that offer an ideal jumping-off point for your online research. Links are conveniently organised by country (e.g. England or Australia), race or cultural grouping (e.g. Indian or Afro-Caribbean) and by events like immigration and naturalisation. The only criticism of this tremendous resource is Cyndi's keenness to plug her own books, but this is forgivable given that her site remains a one-woman show.

---

## Family research portals

### Genealogy Gateway       www.gengateway.com

Steve Lacy's professional looking site has a range of subject-specific areas to help you focus your search – and you can look at surname listings, site listings, or the entire database. Useful online guides lead you to interactive message boards, where you can ask and answer questions.

### Genealogy.com       www.genealogy.com

This site does a good job catering for the virgin genealogist, with a 'Learn About Genealogy' section that contains step-by-step instructions on how to begin researching your family tree, how to organise what you find and where to begin filling the gaps. Seasoned searchers will like the interactive lessons written by research professionals, and it's also a useful place to find out if someone already collected information about your family. If you have an unusual name and relations in the USA or Europe, there's a good chance you'll be able to find them here.

### Genealogy Pages       www.genealogypages.com

A useful destination-packed portal designed like a directory, with links to US resources on military service, pension, and war records. There's also a special area for ethnic groups, and contact details for international genealogical associations.

### The Society of Genealogists       www.sog.org.uk

A unique combination of research material, guidance and support. Check here to find out what you are looking for is in the Society's library – the most comprehensive in the British Isles, with a large collection of family histories, civil registration and census material, and the widest collection of Parish Register copies in the country (over 9,000).

## Databases

*Today's genealogist has a huge choice of high-powered Internet databases to search for ancestors – professional, mostly commercial concerns that will charge for some services.*

### Ancestry.com                                        www.ancestry.com

The US market leader, with thousands of fully searchable directories containing information on hundreds of millions of individuals; by the end of 2000, they expect to have over a billion searchable records on the site. Subscription to this rapidly expanding site costs $59.95 a year.

The site also holds the 'World Tree' – a growing collection of user-submitted family trees – that can be accessed for free. Usefully, the site lets family members all around the world simultaneously collaborate on family histories by storing their research online.

### BT Archive                                        www.bt.com/archives

Near-complete sets of UK telephone directories dating back to 1880, the year after the public telephone service was introduced into Great Britain. Fascinating stuff for all family historians.

### The Commonwealth War Graves Commission    www.cwgc.org

Personal and service details and last resting places for the 1.7 million members of the Commonwealth forces who died in the First and Second World Wars. Here you can identify the cemetery plot or memorial panel where any given name is commemorated. Even if you are simply searching for namesakes that died in the wars, this is a tremendously humbling experience.

**Familia**                                    **www.earl.org.uk/familia**

If you're looking for family history materials in British and Irish public libraries, start here. There's plenty of advice, guidance and suggestions here too.

**FamilyHistory.com**                          **www.familyhistory.com**

Free family history message boards where genealogists around the world can share and exchange information. A vibrant international community that's especially useful for those looking for information on surnames, geographic areas and specific topics.

**FamilySearch**                               **www.familysearch.org**

Behind 700 feet of granite and six huge doors, the Mormons have hidden away the world's biggest collection of genealogical material: more than 2 million microfilm reels of parish records, marriage indexes, census reports and piles of other documents dating back to the Middle Ages. Luckily they are happy to let genealogists rummage in the archives for free. They also collect family trees. Send yours in and the Mormons will preserve it forever.

**Gendex**                                     **www.gendex.com**

A mighty index of nearly 4,000 online databases with a total of 390,000 surnames and nearly 13 million people. Some useful information is free, but to access in-depth data you have to buy 'information credits'. A demonstration mode lets you try before you buy.

**Genealogy Online**                           **www.genealogy.org**

One of the longest established services, this site has been helping family researchers since 1994 with a multitude of free services. The vast majority of the data found here is contributed by the public, whose contributions are eagerly canvassed here.

**GenForum**                                   **http://genforum.genealogy.com**

Discussion and information-sharing forums for 16,000 surnames, with more than 2.5 million messages archived. You can set up your own list of surname forums to follow, post to the forum, or get the email address of the person whose post interests you.

### The Public Record Office (PRO)    www.pro.gov.uk/genealogy

The British government's official archive enables you to trace the service records of an ancestor in the army before 1914 and browse merchant seaman, navy and Metropolitan Police records. The record of immigrants section is particularly strong; emigration (including convicts sent to Australia) is less fully treated, and there is no central index of names. There's a useful quick checklist to get you started on your genealogy search. For a similar service in the US see the Genealogy Research pages at the National Archives (www.nara.gov/genealogy).

### Rootsweb    www.rootsweb.com

Claims to be the Internet's oldest and largest genealogy community. This refreshingly ad-free site offers basic tutorials and access to the Rootsweb Surname list, which contains research and contact links for more than 600,000 names. Helpful articles include topics like 'how to work out if someone's trying to sell you a fake history of your family.'

### The WorldGenWeb Project    www.worldgenweb.org

Non-profit organisation dedicated to make access to genealogical information completely free to all. They haven't succeeded yet.

---

### Newsgroups and mailing lists

---

*If you reach a dead end in your research, you can always ask for help on the web by posting a question to a newsgroup or a mailing list. You may be surprised at the excellent results such an enquiry can produce, however obscure the subject.*

*For discussions on topics relating to the British Isles in general, the two newsgroups associated with the UK & Ireland Genealogical Information Service (www.genuki.org.uk) are particularly useful.*

*They are soc.genealogy.britain and soc.genealogy.ireland, mirrored by their respective mailing lists, genbrit-l and genire-l.*

**Genealogy Mailing Lists** http://lists.rootsweb.com
A definitive source of genealogy newsgroups, with a complete index to several thousand Rootsweb genealogy mailing lists.

**The Society of Genealogists** www.sog.org.uk/online/
**mailing list** lists.html#news
Open to anybody interested in the activities of the Society. The list is used to post notices about and for comments on UK genealogical issues.

*There are a large number of Usenet newsgroups devoted to genealogy topics. The following are a selection of the most useful:*

**alt.genealogy** – general genealogy topics

**alt.scottish.clans** – find your tartan

**soc.genealogy.african** – back to your roots

**soc.genealogy.australia+nz** – Australian and New Zealand genealogy

**soc.genealogy.britain** – British families

**soc.genealogy.india** – find out about nan

**soc.genealogy.ireland** – ah yes, the Muck Malones

**soc.genealogy.surnames** – compare monickers

**soc.genealogy.west-indies** – Caribbean stories

---

**Scottish family research**

---

**Origins.net** www.origins.net
Scottish birth, deaths and marriage databases searchable for a fee. At present, the site contains nearly 30 million index entries to the registers of births/baptisms and marriages from 1553 to 1899 and of deaths for 1855 to 1924.

**The Gathering of the Clans**     www.tartans.com/genalogy.htm
Hoots mon. There are 2,200 surnames here, belonging to more than 100 Scottish Clans. If a surname is associated with more than one Clan, there will be multiple entries of the surname in the Clan Finder list.

**The Scottish Genealogy Society**     www.sol.co.uk/s/scotgensoc
If you join the society, your questions will be answered providing the information is readily available in the Library, but the site will not carry out detailed research.

---

### Irish family research

**Gen.ie**     www.ireland.com/ancestor
This site's excellent surname search will tell the story of how your surname came into being, give variants or related names, show published or printed family histories and outline the distribution of the surname as recorded in 1890.

**Clans of Ireland**     www.irishclans.com/genealogy.html
Conduct your own research or (for a fee) ask them to investigate two ancestral lines of the family of your choice.

**Irish Genealogical Society**     www.rootsweb.com/~irish
Data here includes church records, census substitutes, cemetery lists, and Irish surname information, and the site tries to put members in touch with others researching the same surnames.

**The A to Z of**     www.irish-insight.com/
**Irish Genealogy**     a2z-genealogy/index.html
A-Z of more than 600 lovingly compiled Irish Genealogy resources. Unfortunately these are not all on the same page.

---

### Australia and New Zealand

**Aboriginal and Torres Strait**     www.naa.gov.au/
**Islander Peoples**     gene/atsip.htm

The National Archives of Australia offer this guide to the scant records available on indigenous Australians.

**Australian family history and**          **www.nla.gov.au/**
**genealogy on the Internet**          **oz/genelist.html**
Aussie government site packed with general resources for people researching their family history.

**Australian Institute of**          **www.alphalink.com.**
**Genealogical Studies**          **au/~aigs**
Plenty of hints and advice from this voluntary organisation that encourages the study of genealogy, heraldry and family history.

**AustraliaGenWeb**          **www.rootsweb.com/~auswgw**
Entirely run by volunteers, this rather clunky site offers the usual range of services plus transcripts of vital records. Worth a visit.

**Cemetery Records Online**     **www.interment.net/aus/index.htm**
Australian family graves.

**The Family Ancestral Search Time.**     **www.hsi.com.au**
FAST is a database of over 1.7 million Australian and overseas historical records useful for family history research. Access costs $45 a year.

**First Families 2001**     **www.firstfamilies2001.net.au**
Quirky directory that sets out to list the earliest person in any given family known to have lived in Australia.

**New Zealand Bound**     **www2.symet.net/whitehouse/nzbound**
Want to know which ship brought your ancestor arrived to New Zealand? This specialist site might have the answer.

**New Zealand Genealogy**          **http://downtown.co.nz/**
**Search Engine**          **genealogy**
Search all the online New Zealand passenger lists, family trees, surname interest and other genealogical pages at once.

**New ZealandGenWeb**          www.rootsweb.com/~nzlwgw
Genealogical information and resources for New Zealand.

___

### Canada

**Canadian Genealogy**          www.islandnet.com/~jveinot/
**and History Links**                    cghl/cghl.html
Comprehensive links for Canadian researchers.

**Canadian Genealogy**          www.50megs.com/genealogy/
**Links**                                       canada.html
Canadian and worldwide genealogy links searchable by province,
an all surname genealogy chat room, and a family histories section.

**Cemetery Records Online**    www.interment.net/can/index.htm
Online burial records and tombstone inscriptions of Canadian
cemeteries.

**inGeneas**                              www.ingeneas.com/ingeneas
Canadian passenger and immigration records from the 18th, 19th
and early 20th century.

___

### Jewish genealogy

**JewishGen**                                        www.jewishgen.org
Records might be sparse and hard to dig up, but it can be done.
This is the first stop for Jewish family historians worldwide, with
a discussion group, a database of over 180,000 surnames and
towns and an online Family Tree which contains details of over one
million people.

**The Jewish Genealogical**          www.jgsgb.
**Society of Great Britain**                  ort.org
Records of Britain's Jewish community, and the chance to share
information with other interested parties.

# //GLOSSARY

**ADSL (Asymmetric Digital Subscriber Line)** Technology that allows ten times more data to be sent over the existing copper telephone lines than a conventional modem.

**AOL** One of the biggest Internet companies in the world, with more than 22 million members.

**applet** A program designed to be executed from within another application. They are used for small Internet applications accessible from a browser (like pop-up windows).

**archive** The place on an Internet site where files are stored. It is also a file that contains a number of compressed files.

**attachment** A file attached to an email message. You can attach files through almost any popular email program.

**backbone** The Internet's high-speed data highway and the main network connections that make up the Internet.

**bandwidth** The amount of data that can be transmitted in a fixed amount of time. Used to measure the time it takes for a webpage to fully load.

**bit** Short for binary digit, the smallest unit of information in a computer file.

**bounce** To return email to the sender because it cannot reach its recipient.

**bookmark** To mark a webpage for later retrieval. Nearly all Web browsers support a bookmarking feature. Bookmarks are also known as 'Favorites'. See page 5.

**Boolean operators** System for searching by using and combining terms such as **AND**, **OR**, and **NOT** to sort data. See pages 21-22.

**broadband** Data transmission system in which a single wire carries several channels, or streams of information, at once.

**browser** Program, such as Microsoft Internet Explorer or Netscape Navigator, used to access and display pages on the World Wide Web.

**byte** Abbreviation for binary term, a unit of storage capable of holding a single character. A byte is equal to **8** bits.

**cache** High-speed storage mechanism which stores previously viewed web pages.

**chat** Real-time online conversation between two or more computer users.

**client** An application that runs on a personal computer and relies on a server to perform operations.

**communities** Areas on the Internet which cater for people with common interests, providing a bulletin board and other facilities for them to share news and information.

**compression** Making computer data smaller so less is needed to represent the same information.

**cookie** Tiny file sent to a browser by a web server when a site is accessed. The browser stores the message and it is sent back to the server each time the user returns requests a page from the server. Cookies help websites to track users and store their preferences; they are usually harmless and helpful.

**cyberspace** The virtual, digital world constructed by computer networks.

**database** Collection of information organised so that a computer program can quickly select desired pieces of data; an electronic filing system.

**dial-up** Connection from your computer to the host/server over standard telephone lines.

**directory** A hierarchical structure of files or an organised list of web links.

**domain** Group of computers and devices on a network that are administered as a unit. The UK commercial domain, for example, carries the suffix .co.uk, while US educational institutions have the suffix .edu.

**download** To copy data from an online source to your computer.

**encryption** A way of making data unreadable to everyone except the receiver by way of a secret code.

**FAQ (Frequently Asked Questions)** Document that attempts to answer the most popular questions about any topic.

**favorite** see bookmark.

**filter** Program that accepts certain types of data and refuses others. A mail filter, for example, can block or sort messages according to the name of the sender or the subject matter.

**firewall** A device used to prevent unauthorised Internet users from accessing private networks.

**flame** A newsgroup message in which the writer attacks another participant in harsh, often personal, terms.

**Flash** Advanced downloadable animation technology, used in many design-heavy websites.

**forums** Online discussion group where participants with common interests can exchange open messages.

**frames** The simultaneous loading of two or more web pages at the same time within the same screen.

**freeware** Software given away for free by the author.

**FTP (File Transfer Protocol)** The common procedure used for downloading and uploading files over the Internet.

**gated** Non-public access websites (usually available for a fee).

**GIF (Graphics Interchange Format)** Standard file format for web pictures and graphics – preferred by webmasters because the files are small and download quickly.

**hacker** Individual who gains unauthorised access to computer systems in order to steal or corrupt data.

**hard drive** The internal magnetic disk on which your computer stores data.

**header** The part of an email that precedes the text and contains the message's origin, time of sending and subject lines.

**hierarchy** Category of newsgroups.

**history** In a browser program, previously viewed pages.

**hits** Data matches recorded by search engines and websites.

**home page** The front page on a website that serves as the starting point for navigation, or a site that loads on your browser every time you launch it.

**host** Computer that functions as the beginning and end point of data transfers.

**HTML (Hyper Text Markup Language)** Authoring language used to create documents on the World Wide Web.

**HTTP (HyperText Transfer Protocol)** Underlying protocol used by the web.

**Hypertext** System in which objects can be creatively linked to each other.

**IE (Internet Explorer)** Microsoft's web browser.

**intranet** Private network inside a company or organisation.

**IP (Internet Protocol)** System that enables information to be transferred from one network or computer to another.

**IRC (Internet Relay Chat)** Live chat area where real-time conversations (in the form of text) take place online.

**ISDN (Integrated Services Digital Network)** Data transfer system that sends data three times faster than today's fastest modems.

**ISP (Internet Service Provider)** Middleman who enables individual users to connect the Internet backbone.

**Java** Programming language that includes functions such as animations, calculators, and other fancy tricks.

**JPEG (Joint Photographic Experts Group)** Compression technique for colour images. Files using this method have the suffix .jpg.

**Kbps** Kilobits per second, a measure of data transfer speed.

**keyword** A word entered in a search box by a user, or a word used by web developers to help search engines index websites.

**mailing list** Discussion forum where participants subscribe and receive messages by email.

**metasearch** To search several search engines or directories simultaneously. See page 35.

**moderated** Describes a newsgroup or mailing list monitored by an individual who has the authority to block inappropriate or off-topic messages.

**MPEG (Moving Picture Experts Group)** Method used to compress sound and video into small files. MPEG files bear the suffix .mpg.

**MP3** File format used for high-quality sound files.

**netiquette** Guidelines for posting messages to newsgroups, sending emails and talking in chat rooms. There's a good basic guide at **http://www .albion.com/netiquette**.

**Netscape** Navigator Netscape's web browser program.

**network** Two or more computers that are connected.

**newbie (slang)** A new Internet user.

**newsgroup** Part of the Internet which allows users to post and reply to messages from other users. See page 40.

**Newsreader** Program that enables you to read and post messages to Internet newsgroups.

**offline** Not connected to the Internet.

**online** Connected to the Internet.

**operating system** The program that runs your computer.

**packet** Chunk of data sent across a network.

**packet switching** Key technology used to send data around the Internet: it breaks up a long document into packets for transmission and sends them separately to their destination, where they are reassembled into the original file.

**parameters** Commands used to customise your search.

**password** A word or code used to protect against unauthorised access to data.

**platform** The underlying hardware or software for any system.

**plug-in** A smaller add-on computer program which works in conjunction with a larger application.

**POP (Post Office Protocol)** Standard used to retrieve and send email to and from a mail server.

**portal** Website that offers a range of resources and services.

**post** A message published in a newsgroup or on a bulletin board; also the process of posting that message.

**protocol** Agreed process to enable computers talk to each other on a network.

**register** Giving your details to a site in order to use it or to access extra facilities. Registration can sometimes involve paying a fee.

**results** Returns generated by a search engine.

**search engine** Sophisticated software that searches the Internet for you. See Chapter 2.

**server** Any computer in a network shared by multiple users.

**shareware** Software available for downloading on the Internet that you can try before you buy.

**snail mail** Normal postal mail.

**spam** To send copies of the same message to large numbers of newsgroups or email addresses. Spammers use the Internet to advertise products.

**spider** Search engine program that prowls the Internet looking for new resources.

**subscribe** To join a newsgroup or mailing list. To leave, you have to 'unsubscribe'.

**ticker** Rolling information found on financial news sites.

**URL (Uniform Resource Locator)** Address used to identify the location of all documents and other resources on the Internet.

**Usenet** Public-access network on the Internet that acts as a giant, dispersed bulletin board.

**Zines** Electronic magazine – a website that is loosely modelled after a print magazine.

# //INDEX

# //NOTES

Also published in the Virgin Internet Guide series...

**The Virgin Guide to the Internet**
The advice you need to plug in, log on and get going.

**The Virgin Family Internet Guide**
The only book that lets your family get the best out of the Internet
– and lock out the worst.

**The Virgin Internet Shopping Guide**
You can now buy almost anything on the Internet, and this book
shows you how.

**The Virgin Internet Travel Guide**
The complete guide to choosing your destination
– and getting the best deal online.

**The Virgin Internet Money Guide**
Get your personal finances sorted – online.

**The Virgin Internet Business Guide**
The essential companion for anyone in business.

Coming soon:

**The Virgin Weird Internet Guide**
Strange and wonderful places to surf.

**The Virgin Internet Auction Guide**
Bid for a bargain.

**The Virgin Internet Guide for Kids**
One for the youngsters.

For more information, ask your friendly local bookseller – or check
out our website: **http://www.virgin-books.com**